D.L. MOODY

ON THE 10 COMMANDMENTS

By

D. L. MOODY

"TEKEL: Thou art weighed in the balances,
and art found wanting."

MOODY PRESS

CHICAGO

© 1896 by
THE MOODY BIBLE INSTITUTE
OF CHICAGO

Originally published as
Weighed and Wanting.

ISBN: 0-8024-1778-7

1977 Edition

Moody Press, a ministry of the Moody Bible Institute, is designed for education, evangelization and edification. If we may assist you in knowing more about Christ and the Christian life, please write us without obligation to: Moody Press, c/o MLM, Chicago, Illinois 60610.

Printed in the United States of America

Contents

	PAGE
The Ten Commandments	5
Weighed in the Balances	7
The First Commandment	18
The Second Commandment	29
The Third Commandment	38
The Fourth Commandment	47
The Fifth Commandment	64
The Sixth Commandment	74
The Seventh Commandment	81
The Eighth Commandment	90
The Ninth Commandment	99
The Tenth Commandment	107
The Handwriting Blotted Out	121

3

The Ten Commandments

1. Thou shalt have no other gods before me.
2. Thou shalt not make unto thee any graven image, or any likeness of any thing that is in heaven above, or that is in the earth beneath, or that is in the water under the earth. Thou shalt not bow down thyself to them, nor serve them: for I the LORD thy God am a jealous God, visiting the iniquity of the fathers upon the children unto the third and fourth generation of them that hate me; and shewing mercy unto thousands of them that love me, and keep my commandments.
3. Thou shalt not take the name of the LORD thy God in vain; for the LORD will not hold him guiltless that taketh his name in vain.
4. Remember the sabbath day, to keep it holy. Six days shalt thou labour, and do all thy work: but the seventh day is the sabbath of the LORD thy God: in it thou shalt not do any work, thou, nor thy son, nor thy daughter, thy manservant, nor thy maidservant, nor thy cattle, nor thy stranger that is within thy gates: for in six days the LORD made heaven and earth, the sea, and all that in them is, and rested the seventh day:

5

wherefore the LORD blessed the sabbath day, and hallowed it.

5. Honour thy father and thy mother: that thy days may be long upon the land which the LORD thy God giveth thee.

6. Thou shalt not kill.

7. Thou shalt not commit adultery.

8. Thou shalt not steal.

9. Thou shalt not bear false witness against thy neighbor.

10. Thou shalt not covet thy neighbour's house, thou shalt not covet thy neighbour's wife, nor his manservant, nor his maidservant, nor his ox, nor his ass, nor anything that is thy neighbour's.

Weighed in the Balances

IN THE FIFTH CHAPTER of Daniel we read the history of King Belshazzar. One chapter tells us all we know about him. One short sight of his career is all we have. He bursts in upon the scene and then disappears.

THE EASTERN FEAST

We are told that he made a great feast to a thousand of his lords and drank wine before them. In those days a feast in Eastern countries would sometimes last for six months. How long this feast had been going on we are not told, but in the midst of it, he "commanded to bring the golden and silver vessels which his father Nebuchadnezzar had taken out of the temple which was in Jerusalem; that the king, and his princes, his wives, and his concubines, might drink therein. Then they brought the golden vessels that were taken out of the temple of the house of God which was at Jerusalem; and the king, and his princes, his wives, and his concubines, drank in them. They drank wine, and praised the gods of gold, and of silver, of brass, of iron, of wood, and of stone."

While this impious act was being committed, "in the same hour came forth fingers of a man's hand,

and wrote over against the candlestick upon the plaister of the wall of the king's palace; and the king saw the part of the hand that wrote." We are not told at what hour of the day or the night it happened. Perhaps it was midnight. Perhaps nearly all the guests were more or less under the influence of drink; but they were not so drunk but that they suddenly became sober as they saw something that was supernatural—a handwriting on the wall, right over the golden candlestick.

Every face turned deathly pale "The king's countenance was changed, and his thoughts troubled him, so that the joints of his loins were loosed, and his knees smote one against another." In haste he sent for his wisest men to come and read that handwriting on the wall. They came in one after another and tried to make it out; but they could not interpret it. The king promised that whoever could read it should be made the third ruler in the kingdom; that he should have gifts, and that a gold chain should be put around his neck. But the wise men tried in vain. The king was greatly troubled.

At last, in the midst of the consternation, the queen came in, and she told the monarch, if he would only send for one who used to interpret the dreams of Nebuchadnezzar, he could read the writing and tell him the interpretation thereof. So Daniel was sent for. He was very familiar with it. He knew his Father's handwriting.

"This is the writing that was written, *Mene, Mene, Tekel, Upharsin.* This is the interpretation of the thing: *Mene*—God hath numbered thy kingdom and finished it. *Tekel*—Thou art weighed in the balances and art found wanting. *Peres*—Thy kingdom is divided, and given to the Medes and Persians" (Dan 5:25-28).

If someone had told the king an hour before that the time had come when he must step into the balances and be weighed, he would have laughed at the thought. But the vital hour had come.

The weighing was soon over. The verdict was announced, and the sentence carried out. "In that night was Belshazzar the king of the Chaldeans slain. And Darius the Mede took the kingdom" (Dan 5:30-31). Darius and his army came marching down those streets. There was a clash of arms. Shouts of war and victory rent the air. That night the king's blood mingled with the wine of the banquet hall. Judgment came upon him unexpectedly, suddenly: and probably ninety-nine out of every hundred judgments come in this way. Death comes upon us unexpectedly; it comes upon us suddenly.

Perhaps you say: "I hope Mr. Moody is not going to compare me with that heathen king."

I tell you that a man who does evil in these gospel days is far worse than that king. We live in a land of Bibles. You can get the New Testament for a nickel, and if you haven't got a nickel, you can get it for nothing. Many societies will be glad to give it to you free. We live in the full blaze of Calvary. We live on this side of the cross, but Belshazzar lived more than five hundred years on the other side. He never heard of Jesus Christ. He never heard about the Son of God. He never heard about God except, perhaps, in connection with his father's remarkable vision. He probably had no portion of the Bible, and if he had, probably he didn't believe it. He had no godly minister to point Him to the Lamb of God.

Don't tell me that you are better than that king. I believe that he will rise in judgment and condemn many of us.

All this happened long centuries ago. Let us get down to this century, to this year, to ourselves. We will come to the present time. Let us imagine that now, while I am preaching, down come some balances from the throne of God. They are fastened to the very throne itself. It is a throne of equity, of justice. You and I must be weighed. I venture to say this would be a very solemn audience. There would be no trifling. There would be no indifference. No one would be thoughtless.

Some people have their own balances. A great many are making balances to be weighed in. But after all we must be weighed in God's balances, the balances of the sanctuary. It is a favorite thing with infidels to set their own standard, to measure themselves by other people. But that will not do in the Day of Judgment. Now we will use God's law as a balance weight. When men find fault with the lives of professing Christians, it is a tribute to the law of God.

"Tekel." It is a very short text. It is so short I am sure you will remember it: and that is my object, just to get people to remember God's own Word.

GOD'S HANDWRITING

Let me call your attention to the fact that God wrote on the tables of stone at Sinai as well as on the wall of Belshazzar's palace.

These are the only messages to men that God has written with His own hand. He wrote the commandments out twice, and spoke them aloud in the hearing of Israel.

If it were known that God Himself were going to speak once again to man, what eagerness and excitement there would be! For nearly nineteen hundred years He has been silent. No inspired message has been added to the Bible for nearly nineteen hundred years. How eagerly all men would listen if God should speak once more. Yet men forget that the Bible is God's own Word, and that it is as truly His message today as when it was delivered of old. The law that was given at Sinai has lost none of its solemnity. Time cannot wear out its authority or the fact of its authorship.

I can imagine someone saying, "I won't be weighed by that law. I don't believe in it."

Now men may cavil as much as they like about other parts of the Bible, but I have never met an honest man that found fault with the Ten Commandments. Infidels may mock the Lawgiver and reject Him who has delivered us from the curse of the law, but they can't help admitting that the commandments are right. Renan said that they are for all nations, and will remain the commandments of God during all the centuries.

If God created this world, He must make some laws to govern it. In order to make life safe we must have good laws; there is not a country the sun shines upon that does not possess laws. Now this is God's law. It has come from on high, and infidels and skeptics have to admit that it is pure. Legislatures nearly all over the world adopt it as the foundation of their legal systems.

"The law of the LORD is perfect, converting the soul: the testimony of the LORD is sure, making wise the simple: the statutes of the LORD are right, rejoicing the heart: the commandment of the LORD is pure, enlightening the eyes (Ps 19:7-8).

Now the question for you and me is—are we keeping these commandments? Have we fulfilled all the requirements of the law? If God made us, as we know He did, He had a right to make that law; and if we don't use it aright it would have been better for us if we had never had it, for it will condemn us. We shall be found wanting. The law is all right, but are we right?

AN INFIDEL'S TESTIMONY

It is related of a clever infidel that he sought an acquaintance with the truths of the Bible, and began to read at the books of Moses. He had been in the habit of sneering at the Bible, and in order to be able to refute arguments brought by Christian men, he made up his mind, as he knew nothing about it, to read the Bible and get some idea of its contents. After he had reached the Ten Commandments, he said to a friend:

"I will tell you what I *used* to think. I supposed that Moses was the leader of a horde of bandits; that, having a strong mind, he acquired great influence over a superstitious people; and that on Mount Sinai he played off some sort of fireworks to the amazement of his ignorant followers, who imagined in their fear and superstition that the exhibition was supernatural. I have been looking into the *nature* of that law. I have been trying to see whether I could add anything to it, or take anything from it, so as to make it better. Sir, I cannot! It is perfect!

"The first commandment directs us to make the Creator the object of our supreme love and reverence. That is right. If He be our Creator, Perserver, and supreme Benefactor, we ought to treat Him, and *none other,* as such. The second forbids idolatry. That certainly is right. The third forbids profanity. The fourth fixes a time for religious worship. If there be a God, He ought surely to be worshiped. It is suitable that there should be an outward homage significant of our inward regard. If God be worshiped, it is proper that some *time* should be set apart for that purpose, when all may worship Him harmoniously, and without interruption. One day in seven is certainly not too much, and I do not know that it is too little.

"The fifth commandment defines the peculiar duties arising from family relations. Injuries to our neighbor are then *classified* by the moral law. They are divided into offenses against life, chastity, property, and character; and I notice that the greatest offense in each class is expressly forbidden. Thus the greatest injury to life is murder; to chastity, adultery; to property, theft; to character, perjury. Now the greatest offense must include the least of the same kind. Murder must include the least of the same kind. Murder must include every injury to life; adultery every injury to purity, and so of the rest. And the moral code is closed and perfected by a com-

mand forbidding every improper *desire* in regard to
our neighbors.

"I have been thinking. Where did Moses get that
law? I have read history. The Egyptians and the
adjacent nations were idolaters; so were the Greeks
and Romans; and the wisest or best Greeks or Romans never gave a code of morals like this. Where
did Moses obtain that law, which surpasses the wisdom and philosophy of the most enlightened ages?
He lived at a period comparatively barbarous; but he
has given a law in which the learning and sagacity
of all subsequent time can detect no flaw. Where
did he obtain it? He could not have soared so far
above his age as to have devised it himself. I am
satisfied where he obtained it. It came down from
heaven. It has convinced me of the truth of the religion of the Bible."

The former infidel remained to his death a firm
believer in the truth of Christianity.

We call it the "Mosaic" law, but it has been well
said that the commandments did not originate with
Moses, nor were they done away with when the Mosaic law was fulfilled in Christ, and many of its ceremonies and regulations abolished. We can find no
trace of the existence of any lawmaking body in those
early times, no parliament, or congress that built up
a system of laws. It has come down to us complete
and finished, and the only satisfactory account is that
which tells us that God Himself wrote the commandments on tables of stone.

BINDING TODAY

Some people seem to think we have got beyond

the commandments. What did Christ say? "Think not that I am come to destroy the law and the prophets; I am not come to destroy but to fulfill. For verily I say unto you, Till heaven and earth pass away, one jot or one tittle shall in no wise pass from the law, till all be fulfilled." The commandments of God given to Moses in the Mount at Horeb are as binding today as ever they have been since the time they were proclaimed in the hearing of the people. The Jews said the law was not given in Palestine (which belonged to Israel), but in the wilderness, because the law was for all nations.

Jesus never condemned the law and the prophets, but He did condemn those who did not obey them. Because He gave new commandments, it does not follow that He abolished the old. Christ's explanation of them made them all the more searching. In His Sermon on the Mount, He carried the principles of the commandments beyond the mere letter. He unfolded them and showed that they embraced more, that they are positive as well as prohibitive. The Old Testament closes with these words: "Remember ye the law of Moses my servant, which I commanded unto him in Horeb for all Israel, with the statutes and judgments. Behold, I will send you Elijah the prophet before the coming of the great and dreadful day of the LORD: and he shall turn the heart of the fathers to the children, and the heart of the children to their fathers, lest I come and smite the earth with a curse" (Mal 4:4-6).

Does that look as if the law of Moses was becoming obsolete?

The conviction deepens in me with the years that

the old truths of the Bible must be stated and restated in the plainest possible language. I do not remember ever to have heard a sermon preached on the commandments. I have an index of two thousand five hundred sermons preached by Spurgeon, and not one of them selects its text from the first seventeen verses of Exodus 20. The people must be made to understand that the Ten Commandments are still binding, and that there is a penalty attached to their violation. We do not want a gospel of mere sentiment. The Sermon on the Mount did not blot out the Ten Commandments.

When Christ came He condensed the statement of the law into this form: "Thou shalt love the Lord thy God with all thy heart, and with all thy soul, and with all thy mind and with all thy strength . . . [and] thy neighbour as thyself" (Mk 12:30, 31). Paul said: "Love is the fulfilling of the law" (Ro 13:10). But does this mean that the detailed precepts of the Decalogue are superseded and have become back numbers? Does a father cease to give children rules to obey because they love him? Does a nation burn its statute books because the people have become patriotic? Not at all. And yet people speak as if the commandments do not hold for Christians because they have come to love God. Paul said: "Do we then make void the law through faith? God forbid: yea, we establish the law" (Ro 3:31). It still holds good. The Commandments are necessary. So long as we obey, they do not rest heavy upon us; but as soon as we try to break away, we find they are like fences to keep us within bounds. Horses need bridles even after they have been properly broken in.

"We know that the law is good if a man use it lawfully; knowing this, that the law is not made for a righteous man, but for the lawless and disobedient, for the ungodly and for sinners, for unholy and profane, for murderers of fathers and murderers of mothers, for manslayers, for whoremongers, for them that defile themselves with mankind, for menstealers, for liars, for perjured persons, and if there be any other thing that is contrary to sound doctrine" (1 Ti 1:8-10).

Now, my friend, are you ready to be weighed by this law of God? A great many people say that if they keep the commandments they do not need to be forgiven and saved through Christ. But have you kept them? I will admit that if you perfectly keep the commandments, you do not need to be saved by Christ; but is there a man in the wide world who can truly say that he has done this? Young lady, can you say: "I am ready to be weighed by the law"? Can you, young man? Will you step into the scales and be weighed one by one by the Ten Commandments?

Now face these Ten Commandments honestly and prayerfully. See if your life is right, and if you are treating God fairly. God's statutes are just, are they not? If they are right, let us see if we are right. Let us pray that the Holy Ghost may search each one of us. Let us get alone with God and read His law—read it carefully and prayerfully, and ask Him to show us our sins and what He would have us to do.

The First Commandment

Thou shalt have no other gods before me.

My FRIEND, are you ready to be weighed against this commandment? Have you fulfilled, or are you willing to fulfill, all the requirements of this law? Put it into one of the scales, and step into the other. Is your heart set upon God alone? Have you no other God? Do you love Him above father or mother, the wife of your bosom, your children, home or land, wealth or pleasure?

If men were true to this commandment, obedience to the remaining nine would follow naturally. It is because they are unsound in this that they break the others.

FEELING AFTER GOD

Philosophers are agreed that even the most primitive races of mankind reach out beyond the world of matter to a superior Being. It is as natural for man to feel after God as it is for the ivy to feel after a support. Hunger and thirst drive man to seek for food, and there is a hunger of the soul that needs satisfying, too. Man does not need to be commanded to worship, as there is not a race so high or so low in the scale of civilization but has some kind of god. What he needs is to be directed aright.

This is what the first commandment is for. Before we can worship intelligently, we must know what or whom to worship. God does not leave us in ignorance. When Paul went to Athens, he found an altar dedicated to "The Unknown God," and he proceeded to tell of Him whom we worship. When God gave the commandments to Moses, He commenced with a declaration of His own character, and demanded exclusive recognition. "I am the Lord thy God, which have brought thee out of the land of Egypt, out of the house of bondage. Thou shalt have no other gods before me" (Ex 20:2-3).

Dr. Dale says these words have great significance. The Jews "knew Jehovah as the God who had held back the waves like a wall while they fled across the sea to escape the vengeance of their enemies; they knew Him as the God who had sent thunder, and lightning, and hail, plagues on cattle, and plagues on men, to punish the Egyptians and to compel them to let the children of Israel go; they knew Him as the God whose angel had slain the firstborn of their oppressors, and filled the land from end to end with death, and agony, and terror. He was the same God, so Moses and Aaron told them, who by visions and voices, in promises and precepts, had revealed Himself long before to Abraham, Isaac, and Jacob. We learn what men are from what they say and from what they do. A biography of Luther gives us a more vivid and trustworthy knowledge of the man than the most philosophical essay on his character and creed. The story of his imprisonment and of his journey to Worms, his Letters, his Sermons, and his Table Talk, are worth more than the most elaborate speculations about him. The Jews learned what God is, not from theological dissertations on the Divine attributes, but from the facts of a Divine history. They knew Him for themselves in His own acts and in His own words."

Someone asked an Arab: "How do you know that there is a God?" "How do I know whether a man or a camel passed my tent last night?" he replied. God's footprints in nature and in our own experience are the best evidence of His existence and character.

ISRAELITES EXPOSED TO DANGER

Remember to whom this commandment was given, and we shall see further how necessary it was. The forefathers of the Israelites had worshiped idols, not many generations back. They had recently been delivered out of Egypt, a land of many gods. The Egyptians worshiped the sun, the moon, insects, animals, etc. The ten plagues were undoubtedly meant by God to bring confusion upon many of their sacred objects. The children of Israel were going up to take possession of a land that was inhabited by heathen, who also worshiped idols. There was therefore great need of such a commandment as this. There could be no right relationship between God and man in those days any more than today, until man understood that he must recognize God alone, and not offer Him a divided heart.

If He created us, He certainly ought to have our homage. Is it not right that He should have the first and only place in our affections?

No Compromise

This is one matter in which no toleration can be shown. Religious liberty is a good thing, within certain limits. But it is one thing to show toleration to those who agree on essentials, and another, to those who differ on fundamental beliefs. They were willing to admit any god to the Roman Pantheon. One reason the early Christians were persecuted was that they would not accept a place for Jesus Christ there. Napoleon is said to have entertained the idea of having separate temples in Paris for every known religion, so that every stranger should have a place of worship when attracted toward that city. Such plans are directly opposed to the divine one. God sounded no uncertain note in this commandment. It is plain, unmistakable, uncompromising.

We may learn a lesson from the way a farmer deals with the little shoots that spring up around the trunk of an apple tree. They look promising, and one who has not learned better might welcome their growth. But the farmer knows that they will draw the life-sap from the main tree, injuring its prospects so that it will produce inferior fruit. He therefore takes his axe and his hoe, and cuts away these suckers. The tree then gives a more plentiful and finer crop.

God's Pruning-knife

"Thou shalt not" is the pruning-knife that God uses. From beginning to end, the Bible calls for wholehearted allegiance to Him. There is to be no compromise with other gods.

It took long years for God to impress this lesson upon the Israelites. He called them to be a chosen nation. He made them a peculiar people. But you will notice in Bible history that they turned away from Him continually, and were punished with plague, pestilence, war, and famine. Their sin was not that they renounced God altogether, but that they wanted to worship other gods beside Him. Take the case of Solomon as an example of the whole nation. He married heathen wives who turned away his heart after other gods, and built high places for their idols, and lent countenance to their worship. That was the history of frequent turnings of the whole nation away from God, until finally He sent them into captivity in Babylon and kept them there for seventy years. Since then the Jews have never turned to other gods.

Hasn't the church to contend with the same difficulty today? There are very few who in their hearts do not believe in God, but what they will not do is give Him exclusive right of way. Missionaries tell us that they could easily get converts if they did not require them to be baptized, thus publicly renouncing their idols. Many a person in our land would become a Christian if the gate was not so strait. Christianity is too strict for them. They are not ready to promise full allegiance to God alone. Many a professing Christian is a stumbling block because his worship is divided. On Sunday he worships God; on week-days God has little or no place in his thoughts.

FALSE GODS IN AMERICA TODAY

You don't have to go to heathen lands today to

find false gods. America is full of them. Whatever
you make most of is your god. Whatever you love
more than God is your idol. Many a man's heart is
like some Kafirs' huts, so full of idols that there is
hardly room to turn around. Rich and poor, learned
and unlearned, all classes of men and women are
guilty of this sin. "The mean man boweth down, and
the great man humbleth himself" (Is 2:9).

A man may make a god of himself, of a child, of a
mother, of some precious gift that God has bestowed
upon him. He may forget the Giver and let his heart
go out in adoration toward the gift.

Many make a god of pleasure; that is what their
hearts are set on. If some old Greek or Roman came
to life again and saw man in a drunken debauch,
would he believe that the worship of Bacchus had
died out? If he saw the streets of our large cities
filled with harlots, would he believe that the worship
of Venus had ceased?

Others take fashion as their god. They give their
time and thought to dress. They fear what others
will think of them. Do not let us flatter ourselves
that all idolaters are in heathen countries.

With many it is the god of money. We haven't got
through worshiping the golden calf yet. If a man will
sell his principles for gold, isn't he making it a god?
If he trusts in his wealth to keep him from want and
to supply his needs, are not riches his god? Many a
man says, "Give me money, and I will give you heav-
en. What care I for all the glories and treasures of
heaven? Give me treasures here! I don't care for
heaven! I want to be a successful businessman."
How true are the words of Job: "If I have made gold

my hope, or have said to the fine gold, Thou art my
confidence; if I rejoiced because my wealth was
great, and because mine hand had begotten much; if
I beheld the sun when it shined, or the moon walking
in brightness; and my heart hath been secretly en-
ticed, or my mouth hath kissed my hand: this also
were an iniquity to be punished by the judge: for I
should have denied the God that is above" (Job 31:
24-28).

But all false gods are not as gross as these. There
is *the atheist.* He says that he does not believe in
God; he denies His existence, but he can't help set-
ting up some other god in His place. Voltaire said,
"If there were no God, it would be necessary to in-
vent one." So the atheist speaks of the Great Unknown, the First Cause, the Infinite Mind, etc. Then
there is *the deist.* He is a man who believes in one
God who caused all things; but he doesn't believe in
revelation. He only accepts such truths as can be
discovered by reason. He doesn't believe in Jesus
Christ, or in the inspiration of the Bible. Then there
is *the pantheist,* who says: "I believe that the whole
universe is God. He is in the air, the water, the sun,
the stars"; the liar and the thief included.

Moses' Farewell Message

Let me call your attention to a verse in the thirty-
second chapter of Deuteronomy, thirty-first verse:
"For their rock is not as our Rock, even our enemies
themselves being judges."

These words were uttered by Moses, in his fare-
well address to Israel. He had been with them forty
years. He was their leader and instructor. All the

blessings of heaven came to them through him. And now the old man is about to leave them. If you have never read his speech, do so. It is one of the best sermons in print. I know few sermons in the Old or New Testament that compare with it.

I can see Moses as he delivers this address. His natural activity has not abated. He still has the vigor of youth. His long white hair flows over his shoulders, and his venerable beard covers his breast. He throws down the challenge: "Their rock is not as our Rock, even our enemies themselves being judges."

Has the human heart ever been satisfied with these false gods? Can pleasure or riches fill the soul that is empty of God? How about the atheist, the deist, the pantheist? What do they look forward to? Nothing! Man's life is full of trouble; but when the billows of affliction and disappointment are rising and rolling over them, they have no God to call upon. They shall "cry unto the gods unto whom they offer incense: but they shall not save them at all in the time of their trouble" (Jer 11:12). Therefore I contend "their rock is not as our Rock."

My friends, when the hour of affliction comes, they call in a minister to give consolation. When I was settled in Chicago, I used to be called out to attend many funerals. I would inquire what the man was in his belief. If I found out he was an atheist, or a deist, or a pantheist, when I went to the funeral and in the presence of his friends, said one word about that man's doctrine, they would feel insulted. Why is it that in a trying hour, when they have been talking all the time against God—why is it that in the darkness of affliction they call in believers in that God to administer consolation? Why doesn't the atheist preach no hereafter, no heaven, no God in the hour of affliction? This very fact is an admission that "their rock is not as our Rock, even our enemies themselves being judges."

The deist says there is no use in praying, because nothing can change the decrees of deity; God never answers prayer. Is his rock as our Rock?

The Bible is true. There is only one God. How many men have said to me: "Mr. Moody, I would give the world if I had your faith, your consolation, the hope you have with your religion."

Isn't that a proof that their rock is not as our Rock?

Some years ago I went into a man's house, and when I commenced to talk about religion he turned to his daughter and said: "You had better leave the room. I want to say a few words to Mr. Moody." When she had gone, he opened a perfect torrent of infidelity upon me. "Why did you send your daughter out of the room before you said this?" I asked. "Well," he replied, "I did not think it would do her any good to hear what I said."

Is his rock as our Rock? Would he have sent his daughter out if he really believed what he said?

No Consolation Except in God

No. There is no satisfaction for the soul except in the God of the Bible. We come back to Paul's words and get consolation for time and eternity: "We know that an idol is nothing in the world, and that there is none other God but one. For though there be that are called gods, whether in heaven or in earth (as there be gods many, and lords many), but to us there is but one God, the Father, of whom are all things, and we in him; and one Lord Jesus Christ, by whom are all things, and we by him" (1 Co 8:4-6).

My friend, can you say that sincerely? Is all your hope centered on God in Christ? Are you trusting Him alone? Are you ready to step into the scales and be weighed against this first commandment?

WHOLEHEARTED ALLEGIANCE

God will not accept a divided heart. He must be absolute monarch. There is not room in your heart for two thrones. Christ said: "No man can serve two masters: for either he will hate the one, and love the other; or else he will hold to the one, and despise the other. Ye cannot serve God and mammon" (Mt 6: 24). Mark you, He did not say, "No man *shall* serve . . . Ye *shall* not serve" but "No man *can* serve . . . Ye *cannot* serve." That means more than a command; it means that you cannot mix the worship of the true God with the worship of another god any more than you can mix oil and water. It cannot be done. There is not room for any other throne in the heart if Christ is there. If worldliness should come in, godliness would go out.

The road to heaven and the road to hell lead in different directions. Which master will you choose to follow? Be an out-and-out Christian. Him only shall you serve. Only thus can you be well pleasing to God. The Jews were punished with seventy years of captivity because they worshiped false gods. They have suffered nineteen hundred years because they rejected the Messiah. Will you incur God's displeasure by rejecting Christ too? He died to save you. Trust Him with your whole heart, for with the heart man believeth unto righteousness.

I believe that when Christ has the first place in our hearts—when the kingdom of God is first in everything—we shall have power, and we shall not have power until we give Him His rightful place. If we let some false god come in and steal our love away from the God of heaven, we shall have no peace or power.

The Second Commandment

Thou shalt not make unto thee any graven image, or any likeness of any thing that is in heaven above, or that is in the earth beneath, or that is in the water under the earth: thou shalt not bow down thyself to them, nor serve them: for I the Lord thy God am a jealous God, visiting the iniquity of the fathers upon the children unto the third and fourth generation of them that hate me; and shewing mercy unto thousands of them that love me, and keep my commandments.

THE FIRST COMMANDMENT, which we have just considered, points out the one true object of worship; this commandment, is to tell us the right way in which to worship. The former commands us to worship God alone; this calls for purity and spirituality as we approach Him. The former condemns the worship of false gods; this prohibits false forms. It relates more especially to outward acts of worship; but these are only the expression of what is in the heart.

Perhaps you will say that there is no trouble about this weight. We might go off to other ages or other lands and find people who make images and bow down to them; but we have none here. Let us see if this is true. Let us step into the scales and see if we can turn them when weighed against this commandment.

I believe this is where the battle is fought. Satan tries to keep us from worshiping God aright, and from making Him first in everything. If I let some image made by man get into my heart and take the place of God the Creator, it is a sin. I believe that Satan is willing to have us worship anything, however sacred—the Bible, the crucifix, the church—if only we do not worship God Himself.

You cannot find a place in the Bible where a man has been allowed to bow down and worship anyone but the God of heaven and Jesus Christ His Son. In the book of Revelation when an angel came down to John, he was about to fall down and worship him, but the angel would not let him. If an angel from heaven is not to be worshiped, when you find people bowing down to pictures, to images, even when they bow down to worship the cross, *it is a sin.* There are a great many who seem to be carried away with these things. "Thou shalt have no other gods before me." "Thou shalt not bow down thyself to any graven image." God wants us to worship Him only, and if we do not believe that Jesus Christ is God manifest in the flesh we should not worship Him. I have no more doubt about the divinity of Christ than I have that I exist.

Worship involves two things: the internal belief, and the external act. We transgress in our hearts by having a wrong conception of God and of Jesus Christ before ever we give public expression in action. As someone has said, it is wrong to have loose opinions as well as to be guilty of loose practices.

That is what Paul meant when he said: "We ought not to *think* that the Godhead is like unto gold or silver, or stone, graven by art and man's device" (Acts 17:29, italics added). The opinions that some people hold about Christ are not in accordance with the Bible and are real violations of this second commandment.

A QUESTION

The question at once arises—is this commandment intended to forbid the use of drawings and pictures of created things altogether? Some contend that it does. They point to the Jews and the Muslims as a proof. The Jews have never been much given to art. The Muslims to this day do not use designs of animals, etc., in patterns. But I do not agree with them. I think God only meant to forbid images and other representations when these were intended to be used as objects of religious veneration. "Thou shalt not make *unto thee* . . . Thou shalt not *bow down thyself* to them, nor *serve* them." In Exodus we are told that God ordered the bowls of the golden candlestick for the tabernacle to be made "like unto almonds, with a knop and a flower" (Ex 25:33); and the robe of the ephod had a hem on which they were to put a bell and a pomegranate alternately. How could God order something that broke this second commandment?

I believe that this commandment is a call for spiritual worship. It is in line with Christ's declaration to that Samaritan woman, "God is a Spirit: and they that worship him must worship him in spirit and in truth" (Jn 4:24).

This is precisely what is difficult for men to do. The apostles were hardly in their graves before people began to put up images of them, and to worship relics. People have a desire for something tangible, something that they can see. That is why there is a demand for ritualism. Some people are born Puritans; they want a simple form of worship. Others think they cannot get along without forms and ceremonies that appeal to the senses. And many a one whose heart is not sincere before God takes refuge in these forms, and eases his conscience by making an outward show of religion.

The second commandment is to restrain this desire and tendency.

God is grieved when we are untrue to Him. God is love, and He is wounded when our affections are transferred to anything else. The penalty attached to this commandment teaches us that man has to reap what he sows, whether good or bad; and not only that, but his children have to reap with him. Notice that punishment is visited upon the children unto the *third* or the *fourth* generation, while mercy is shown unto thousands, or (as it is more correctly) unto the *thousandth* generation.

THE FOLLY OF IMAGES

Think for a moment, and you will see how idle it is to try to make any representation of God. Christians have tried to paint the Trinity, but how can you depict the invisible? Can you draw a picture of your own soul or spirit or will? Moses impressed it upon Israel that when God spake to them out of the midst of the fire they saw no manner of similitude, but only heard His voice.

A picture or image of God must degrade our conception of Him. It fastens us down to one idea, whereas we ought to grow in grace and in knowledge. It makes God finite. It brings Him down to our level. It has given rise to the horrible idols of India and China, because they fashion these images according to their own notions. How would the president feel if Americans made such hideous objects to resemble him as they make of their gods in heathen countries? Isaiah bore down with tremendous irony upon the folly of idol-makers: upon the smith who fashioned gods with tongs and hammers; and upon the carpenter who took a tree, and used part of it for a fire to warm himself and roast his meat, and made part of it in the figure of a man with his rule and plane and compass, and called it his god and worshiped it. "A deceived heart hath turned him aside."

A man must be greater than anything he is able to make or manufacture. What folly then to think of worshiping such things!

The tendency of the human heart to represent God by something that appeals to the senses is the origin of all idolatry. It leads directly to image-worship. At first there may be no desire to worship the thing itself, but it inevitably ends in that. As Dr. MacLaren says: "Enlisting the senses as allies of the spirit is risky work. They are apt to fight for their own hand when they once begin, and the history of all symbolical and ceremonial worship shows that the experiment is much more likely to end in sensualizing religion than in spiritualizing sense."

PICTURES AND IMAGES

But someone says, "I find pictures are a great help to me, and images. I know that they are not themselves sacred, but they help me in my devotions to fix my thoughts on God."

When Dr. Trumbull was in Northfield, he used an illustration that is a good answer to this. He said, "Suppose a young man were watching from a window for his absent mother's return, with a wish to catch the first glimpse of her approaching face. Would he be wise or foolish in putting up a photograph of her on the windowframe before him, as a help to bear her in mind as he looks for her coming? As there can be no doubt about the answer to that question, so there can be no doubt that we can best come into communion with God by closing our eyes to everything that can be seen with the natural eye, and opening the eyes of our spirit to the sight of God the Spirit."

I would a great deal sooner have five minutes communion with Christ than spend years before pictures and images of Him. Whatever comes between my soul and my Maker is not a help to me, but a hindrance. God has given different means of grace by which we can approach Him. Let us use these, and not seek for other things that He has distinctly forbidden.

Dr. Dale says that in his college days he had an engraving of our Lord hanging over his mantelpiece. "The calmness, the dignity, the gentleness, and the sadness of the face represented the highest conceptions which I had in those days of the human presence of Christ. I often looked at it, and seldom without being touched by it. I discovered in the course of a few months that the superstitious sentiments were gradually clustering about it, which are always created by the visible representations of the divine. The engraving was becoming to me the shrine of God manifest in the flesh, and I understood the growth of idolatry. The visible symbol is at first a symbol and nothing more; it assists thought; it stirs passion. At last it is identified with the God whom it represents. If, every day, I bow before a crucifix in prayer, if I address it as though it were Christ, though I know it is not, I shall come to feel for it a reverence and love which are of the very essence of idolatry."

Did you ever stop to think that the world has not a single picture of Christ that has been handed down to us from His disciples? Who knows what He was like? The Bible does not tell us how He looked, except in one or two isolated general expressions as when it says, "His visage was so marred more than any man, and his form more than the sons of men." We don't know anything definite about His features, the color of His hair and eyes, and the other details that would help to give a true representation. What artist can tell us? He left no keepsakes to His disciples. His clothes were seized by the Roman soldiers who crucified Him. Not a solitary thing was left to be handed down among His followers. Doesn't it look as if Christ left no relics lest they should be held sacred and worshiped?

History tells us further that the early Christians shrank from making pictures and statues of any kind of Christ. They knew Him as they had seen Him after His resurrection, and had promises of His continued presence that pictures could not make any more real.

I have seen very few pictures of Christ that do not repel me more or less. I sometimes think that it is wrong to have pictures of Him at all.

Speaking of the crucifix Dr. Dale says: "It makes our worship and our prayer unreal. We are adoring a Christ who does not exist. He is not on the cross now, but on the throne. His agonies are past forever. He has risen from the dead. He is at the right hand of God. If we pray to a dying Christ, we are praying not to Christ Himself, but to a mere remembrance of Him. The injury which the crucifix has inflicted on the religious life of Christendom, in encouraging a morbid and unreal devotion, is absolutely incalculable. It has given us a dying Christ instead of a living Christ, a Christ separated from us by many centuries instead of a Christ nigh at hand."

The Indwelling Christ

No one can say that we have nowadays any need of such things. "Behold I stand at the door, and knock: if any man hear my voice, and open the door, I will come in to him, and will sup with him, and he with me." If Christ is in our hearts, why need we set Him before our eyes? "Where two or three gathered together in my name, there am I in the midst of them." If we take hold of that promise by faith, what need is there of outward symbols and reminders? If the King Himself is present, why need we . bow down before statues supposed to represent Him? To fill His place with an image, someone has said, is like blotting the sun out of the heavens and substituting some other light in its place: "You cannot see Him through chinks of ceremonialism; or through the blind eyes of erring man; or by images graven with art and man's device; or in cunningly devised fables of artificial and perverted theology. Nay, seek Him in His own Word, in the revelation of Himself which He gives to all who walk in His ways. So you will be able to keep that admonition of the last word of all the New Testament revelation: 'Little children, keep yourselves from idols' " (1 Jn 5:21).

I believe many an earnest Christian would be found wanting if put in the balances against this commandment. "Tekel" is the sentence that would be written against them, because their worship of God and of Christ is not pure. May God open our eyes to the danger that is creeping more and more into public worship throughout Christendom! Let us ever bear in mind Christ's words in the fourth chapter of John's Gospel, which show that true spiritual worship is not a matter of special times and special places because it is of all times and all places:

"Believe me, the hour cometh, when ye shall neither in this mountain, nor yet at Jerusalem, worship the Father. . . . But the hour cometh, and now is, when the true worshippers shall worship the Father in spirit and truth: for the Father seeketh such to worship him. God is a Spirit: and they that worship him must worship him in spirit and in truth" (Jn 4:21-24).

The Third Commandment

Thou shalt not take the name of the Lord thy God in vain; for the Lord will not hold him guiltless that taketh His name in vain.

I WAS GREATLY AMAZED not long ago in talking to a man who thought he was a Christian, to find that once in a while, when he got angry, he would swear. I said: "My friend, I don't see how you can tear down with one hand what you are trying to build up with the other. I don't see how you can profess to be a child of God and let those words come out of your lips."

He replied: "Mr. Moody, if you knew me you would understand. I have a very quick temper. I inherited it from my father and mother, and it is uncontrollable; but my swearing comes only from the lips."

When God said, "I will not hold him guiltless that takes my name in vain," He meant what He said, and I don't believe anyone can be a true child of God who takes the name of God in vain. What is the grace of God for, if it is not to give me control of my temper so that I shall not lose control and bring down the curse of God upon myself? When a man is born of God, God takes the "swear" out of him.

Make the fountain good, and the stream will be good. Let the heart be right; then the language will be right; the whole life will be right. But no man can serve God and keep His law until he is born of God. There we see the necessity of the new birth.

To take God's name "in vain" means either (1) lightly, without thinking, flippantly; or (2) profanely, deceitfully.

USING GOD'S NAME IRREVERENTLY

I think it is shocking to use God's name with so little reverence as is common nowadays, even among professing Christians. We are told that the Jews held it so sacred that the covenant name of God was never mentioned amongst them except once a year by the high priest on the Day of Atonement, when he went into the holy of holies. What a contrast that is to the familiar use Christians make of it in public and private worship! We are apt to rush into God's presence and rush out again without any real sense of the reverence and awe that is due Him. We forget that we are on holy ground.

Do you know how often the word "reverend" occurs in the Bible? Only once. And what is it used in connection with? God's name. Psalm 11:9: *"holy and reverend is his name."* So important did the Jewish rabbi consider this commandment that they said the whole world trembled when it was first proclaimed on Sinai.

USING GOD'S NAME PROFANELY

But though there is far too much of this frivolous, familiar use of God's name, the commandment is bro-

ken a great deal more by profanity. Taking the name
of God in vain is blasphemy. Is there a swearing
man who reads this? What would you do if you were
put into the balances of the sanctuary, if you had to
step in opposite to this third commandment? Think
a moment. Have you been taking God's name in
vain today?

I do not believe men would ever have been guilty
of swearing unless God had forbidden it. They do
not swear by their friends, their fathers or mothers,
their wives or children. They want to show how they
despise God's law.

A great many men think there is nothing in swearing. Bear in mind that God sees something wrong in
it, and He says He will not hold men guiltless, even
though society does.

I met a man sometime ago who told me he had
never sinned in his life. He was the first perfect man
I had ever met. I thought I would question him, and
began to measure him by the law. I asked him: "Do
you ever get angry?"

"Well," he said, "sometimes I do; but I have a
right to do so. It is righteous indignation."

"Do you swear when you get angry?"

He admitted he did sometimes.

"Then," I asked, "are you ready to meet God?"

"Yes," he replied, "because I never mean anything
when I swear."

Suppose I steal a man's watch and he comes after
me.

"Yes," I say, "I stole your watch and pawned it,
but *I did not mean anything by it.* I pawned it and
spent the money, but *I did not mean anything by it.*"

You would smile at and deride such a statement.

Ah, friends! You cannot trifle with God in that way. Even if you swear without meaning it, it is forbidden by God. Christ said: "Every idle word that men shall speak, they shall give an account thereof in the day of judgment; for by thy words thou shalt be justified, and by thy words thou shalt be condemned" (Mt 12:36, 37). You will be held accountable whether your words are idle or blasphemous.

A SENSELESS HABIT

The habit of swearing is condemned by all sensible persons. It has been called "the most gratuitous of all sins," because no one gains by it; it is "not only sinful, but useless." An old writer said that when the accusing angel, who records men's words, flies up to heaven with an oath, he blushes as he hands it in.

When a man blasphemes, he shows an utter contempt for God. I was in the army during the war, and heard men cursing and swearing. Some godly woman would pass along the ranks looking for her wounded son, and not an oath would be heard. They would not swear before their mothers, or their wives, or their sisters; they had more respect for them than they had for God!

Isn't it a terrible condemnation that swearing held its own until it came to be recognized as a vulgar thing, a sin against society? Men dropped it then, who never thought of its being a sin against God.

There will be no swearing men in the kingdom of God. They will have to drop that sin, and repent of it, before they see the kingdom of God.

How to Keep from Swearing

Men often ask: "How can I keep from swearing?"
I will tell you. If God puts His love into your heart,
you will have no desire to curse Him. If you have
much regard for God, you will no more think of
cursing Him than you would think of speaking lightly
or disparagingly of a mother whom you love. But
the natural man is at enmity with God and has utter contempt for His law. When that law is written
on his heart, there will be no trouble in obeying it.

When I was out west about thirty years ago, I was
preaching one day in the open air, when a man drove
up in a fine turn-out, and after listening a little while
to what I was saying, he put the whip to his fine-look-
ing steed, and away he went, I never expected to see
him again, but the next night he came back, and he
kept on coming regularly night after night.

I noticed that his forehead itched—you have noticed people who keep putting their hands to their
foreheads?—he didn't want any one to see him shed-
ding tears—of course not! It is not a manly thing to
shed tears in a religious meeting, of course!

After the meeting I said to a gentleman: "Who is
that man who drives up here every night? Is he interested?" "Interested! I should think not! You
should have heard the way he talked about you today." "Well," I said, "that is a sign he is interested."

If no man ever has anything to say against you,
your Christianity isn't worth much. Men said of the
Master, "He has a devil," and Jesus said that if they
had called the master of the house Beelzebub, how
much more them of his household.

I asked where this man lived, but my friend told me not to go to see him, for he would only curse me. I said: "It takes God to curse a man; man can only bring curses on his own head." I found out where he lived and went to see him. He was the wealthiest man within a hundred miles of that place, and had a wife and seven beautiful children. Just as I got to his gate I saw him coming out of the front door. I stepped up to him and said: "This is Mr. ——, I believe?"

He said, "Yes, sir; that is my name." Then he straightened up and asked— "What do you want?"

"Well," I said, "I would like to ask you a question, if you won't be angry."

"Well, what is it?"

"I am told that God has blessed you above all men in this part of the country; that He has given you wealth, a beautiful Christian wife, and seven lovely children. I do not know if it is true, but I hear that all He gets in return is cursing and blasphemy."

He said, "Come in; come in." I went in.

"Now," he said, "what you said out there is true. If any man has a fine wife I am the man, and I have a lovely family of children, and God has been good to me. But do you know, we had company here the other night, and I cursed my wife at the table and did not know it till after the company had gone. I never felt so mean and contemptible in my life as when my wife told me of it. She said she wanted the floor to open and let her down out of her seat. If I have tried once, I have tried a hundred times to stop swearing. You preachers don't know anything about it."

"Yes," I said, "I know all about it; I have been a drummer."

"But," he said, "you don't know anything about a businessman's troubles. When he is harassed and tormented the whole time, he can't help swearing."

"Oh, yes," I said, "he can. I know something about it. I used to swear myself."

"What! You used to swear?" he asked; "how did you stop?"

"I never stopped."

"Why, you don't swear now, do you?"

"No; I have not sworn for years."

"How did you stop?"

"I never stopped. It stopped itself."

He said, "I don't understand this."

"No," I said, "I know you don't. But I came up to talk to you, so that you will never want to swear as long as you live."

I began to tell him about Christ in the heart; how that would take the temptation to swear out of a man.

"Well," he said, "how am I to get Christ?"

"Get right down here and tell Him what you want."

"But," he said, "I was never on my knees in my life. I have been cursing all the day, and I don't know how to pray or what to pray for."

"Well," I said, "it is mortifying to have to call on God for mercy when you have never used His name except in oaths; but He will not turn you away. Ask God to forgive you if you want to be forgiven."

Then the man got down and prayed—only a few sentences, but thank God, it is the short prayers, after all, which bring the quickest answers. After he prayed he got up and said: "What shall I do now?"

I said, "Go down to the church and tell the people there that you want to be an out-and-out Christian."

"I cannot do that," he said; "I never go to church except to some funeral."

"Then it is high time for you to go for something else," I said.

After a while he promised to go, but did not know what the people would say. At the next church prayer meeting, the man was there, and I sat right in front of him. He stood up and put his hands on the settee, and he trembled so much that I could feel the settee shake. He said:

"My friends, you know all about me. If God can save a wretch like me, I want to have you pray for my salvation."

That was thirty odd years ago. Sometime ago I was back in that town, and did not see him; but when I was in California, a man asked me to take dinner with him. I told him that I could not do so, for I had another engagement. Then he asked if I remembered him, and told me his name. "Oh," I said, "tell me, have you ever sworn since that night you knelt in your drawing-room, and asked God to forgive you?"

"No," he replied, "I have never had a desire to swear since then. It was all taken away."

He was not only converted, but became an earnest, active Christian, and all these years has been serving God. That is what will take place when a man is born of the divine nature.

Is there a swearing man ready to put this commandment into the scales, and step in to be weighed? Suppose you swear only once in six months or a year—suppose you swear only once in ten years—do you think God will hold you guiltless for the act? It shows that your heart is not clean in God's sight. What are you going to do, blasphemer? Would you not be found wanting? You would be like a feather in the balance.

The Fourth Commandment

Remember the sabbath day, to keep it holy. Six days shalt thou labour, and do all thy work: but the seventh day is the sabbath of the Lord thy God: in it thou shalt not do any work, thou, nor thy son, nor thy daughter, thy manservant, nor thy maidservant, nor thy cattle, nor thy stranger that is within thy gates: for in six days the Lord made heaven and earth, the sea, and all that in them is, and rested the seventh day: wherefore the Lord blessed the sabbath day, and hallowed it.

THERE HAS BEEN an awful letting-down in this country regarding the Sabbath during the last twenty-five years, and many a man has been shorn of spiritual power, like Samson, because he is not straight on this question. Can *you* say that you observe the Sabbath properly? You may be a professed Christian: are you obeying this commandment? Or do you neglect the house of God on the Sabbath day, and spend your time drinking and carousing in places of vice and crime, showing contempt for God and His law? Are you ready to step into the scales? Where were you last Sabbath? How did you spend it?

I honestly believe that this commandment is just as binding today as it ever was. I have talked with

47

men who have said that it has been abrogated, but they have never been able to point to any place in the Bible where God repealed it. When Christ was on earth, He did nothing to set it aside; He freed it from the traces under which the scribes and Pharisees had put it, and gave it its true place. "The sabbath was made for man, not man for the sabbath." It is just as practicable and as necessary for men today as it ever was—in fact, more than ever, because we live in such an intense age.

The Sabbath was binding in Eden, and it has been in force ever since. The fourth commandment begins with the word *remember,* showing that the Sabbath already existed when God wrote this law on the tables of stone at Sinai. How can men claim that this one commandment has been done away with when they will admit that the other nine are still binding?

I believe that the Sabbath question today is a vital one for the whole country. It is the burning question of the present time. If you give up the Sabbath the church goes; if you give up the church the home goes; and if the home goes the nation goes. That is the direction in which we are traveling.

The church of God is losing its power on account of so many people giving up the Sabbath, and using it to promote selfishness.

How to Observe the Sabbath

"Sabbath" means "rest," and the meaning of the word gives a hint as to the true way to observe the day. God rested after creation, and ordained the

Sabbath as a rest for man. He blessed it and hallowed
it. Remember the *rest-day* to keep it holy. It is the
day when the body may be refreshed and strength-
ened after six days of labor, and the soul drawn into
closer fellowship with its Maker.

True observance of the Sabbath may be considered under two general heads: cessation from ordinary secular work, and religious exercises.

1. Cessation From Secular Work

A man ought to turn aside from his ordinary em-
ployment one day in seven. There are many whose
occupation will not permit them to observe Sunday,
but they should observe some other day as a Sabbath.
Saturday is my day of rest, because I generally preach
on Sunday, and I look forward to it as a boy does to
a holiday. God knows what we need.

Ministers and missionaries often tell me that they
take no rest-day; they do not need it because they
are in the Lord's work. That is a mistake. When God
was giving Moses instructions about the building of
the tabernacle, He referred especially to the Sabbath,
and gave injunctions for its strict observance; and
later, when Moses was conveying the words of the
Lord to the children of Israel, he interpreted them
by saying that not even were sticks to be gathered on
the sabbath to kindle fires for smelting or other purposes. In spite of their zeal and haste to erect the
tabernacle, the workmen were to have their day of
rest. The command applies to ministers and others
engaged in Christian work today as much as to those
Israelite workmen of old.

WORKS OF NECESSITY AND OF EMERGENCY

In judging whether any work may or may not be lawfully done on the Sabbath, find out the reason and object for doing it. Exceptions are to be made for works of necessity and works of emergency. By "works of necessity" I mean those acts that Christ justified when He approved of leading one's ox or ass to water. Watchmen, police, stokers on board steamers, and many others have engagements that necessitate their working on the sabbath. By "works of emergency" I mean those referred to by Christ when He approved of pulling an ox or an ass out of a pit on the sabbath day. In case of fire or sickness a man is often called on to do things that would not otherwise be justifiable.

A Christian man was once urged by his employer to work on Sunday. "Does not your Bible say that if your ass falls into a pit on the Sabbath, you may pull him out?" "Yes," replied the other ;"but if the ass had the habit of falling into the same pit every Sabbath, I would either fill up the pit or sell the ass."

Every man must settle the question as it affects unnecessary work, with his own conscience.

No man should make another work seven days in the week. One day is demanded for rest. A man who has to work the seven days has nothing to look forward to, and life becomes humdrum. Many Christians are guilty in this respect.

SABBATH TRAVELING

Take, for instance, the question of Sabbath traveling. I believe we are breaking God's laws by using the cars on Sunday and depriving conductors and others of their Sabbath. Remember, the fourth commandment expressly refers to the "stranger that is within thy gates." Doesn't that touch Sabbath travel?

But you ask, "What are we to do? How are we to get to church?"

I reply, on foot. It will be better for you. Once when I was holding meetings in London, in my ignorance I made arrangements to preach four times in different places one Sabbath. After I had made the appointments I found I had to walk sixteen miles; but I walked it, and I slept that night with a clear conscience. I have made it a rule never to use the cars, and if I have a private carriage, I insist that horse and man shall rest on Monday. I want no hackman to rise up in judgment against me.

My friends, if we want to help the Sabbath, let business men and Christians never patronize cars on the Sabbath. I would hate to own stock in those companies, to be the means of taking the Sabbath from these men, and have to answer for it at the day of judgment. Let those who are Christians at any rate endeavor to keep a conscience void of offense on this point.

SABBATH TRADING

There are many who are inclined to use the Sabbath in order to make money faster. This is no new sin. The prophet Amos hurled his invectives against oppressors who said, "When will the new moon be gone, that we may sell corn? and the sabbath, that we may set forth wheat?"

Covetous men have always chafed under the restraint, but not until the present time do we find that they have openly counted on Sabbath trade to make money. We are told that many street car companies would not pay if it were not for the Sabbath traffic, and the Sabbath edition of newspapers is also counted upon as the most profitable.

The railroad men of this country are breaking down with softening of the brain, and die at the age of fifty or sixty. They think their business is so important that they must run their trains seven days in the week. Businessmen travel on the Sabbath so as to be on hand for business Monday morning. But if they do so God will not prosper them.

Work is good for man and is commanded, "Six days shalt thou labor"; but overwork and work on the Sabbath takes away the best thing he has.

NECESSARY AND BENEFICIAL

The good effect on a nation's health and happiness produced by the return of the Sabbath, with its cessation from work, cannot be overestimated. It is needed to repair and restore the body after six days of work. It is proved that a man can do more in six days than in seven. Lord Beaconsfield said: "Of all divine institutions, the most divine is that which secures a day of rest for man. I hold it to be the most valuable blessing conceded to man. It is the cornerstone of all civilization, and its removal might affect even the health of the people."

Mr. Gladstone recently told a friend that the secret of his long life is that amid all the pressure of public cares he never forgot the Sabbath, with its rest for the body and the soul. The constitution of the United States protects the president in his weekly day of rest. He has ten days, "Sundays excepted," in which to consider a bill that has been sent to him for signature. Every workingman in the republic ought to be as thoroughly protected as the president. If workingmen got up a strike against unnecessary work on the Sabbath, they would have the sympathy of a good many.

"Our bodies are seven-day clocks," says Talmage, "and they need to be wound up, and if they are not wound up they run down into the grave. No man can continuously break the Sabbath and keep his physical and mental health. Ask aged men, and they will tell you they never knew men who continuously broke the Sabbath who did not fail in mind, body, or moral principles."

All that has been said about rest for man is true for working animals. God didn't forget them in this commandment, and man should not forget them either.

2. RELIGIOUS ACTIVITY

But "rest" does not mean idleness. No man enjoys idleness for any length of time. When one goes on a vacation, one does not lie around doing nothing all the time. Hard work at tennis, hunting, and other pursuits fills the hours. A healthy mind must find something to do.

Hence the Sabbath rest does not mean inactivity. "Satan finds some mischief still for idle hands to do." The best way to keep off bad thoughts and to avoid temptation is to engage in active religious exercises.

As regards these, we should avoid extremes. On the one hand we find a rigor in Sabbath observance that is nowhere commanded in Scripture, and that reminds one of the formalism of the Pharisees more than of the spirit of the Gospel. Such strictness does more harm than good. It repels people and makes the Sabbath a burden. On the other hand, we should jealously guard against a loose way of keeping the Sabbath. Already in many cities it is profaned openly.

When I was a boy, the Sabbath lasted from sundown on Saturday to sundown on Sunday, and I remember how we boys used to shout when it was over. It was the worst day in the week to us. I believe it can be made the brightest day in the week. Every child ought to be reared so that he shall be able to say that he would rather have the other six days weeded out of his memory than the Sabbath of his childhood.

PUBLIC WORSHIP

Make the Sabbath a day of religious activity. First of all, of course, is attendance at public worship. "There is a discrepancy," says John McNeill, "between our creed about the Sabbath day and our actual conduct. In many families, at ten o'clock on the Sabbath, attendance at church is still an open question. There is no open question on Monday morning—'John, will you go to work today?'"

A minister rebuked a farmer for not attending church, and said, "You know, John, you are never absent from market."

"Oh," was the reply, "we *must* go to market."

Someone has said that without the Sabbath, the Church of Christ could not, as a visible organization, exist on earth. Another has said that "we need to be in the drill of observance as well as in the liberty of faith." Human nature is so treacherous that we are apt to omit things altogether unless there is some special reason for doing them. A man is not likely to worship at all unless he has regularly appointed times and means for worship. Family and private devotions are almost certain to be omitted altogether unless one gets into the habit and has a special time set apart daily.

A REMINISCENCE

I remember blaming my mother for sending me to church on the Sabbath. On one occasion the preacher had to send someone into the gallery to wake me up. I thought it was hard to have to work in the field all the week and then to be obliged to go to church and hear a sermon I didn't understand. I thought I wouldn't go to church any more when I got away from home; but I had got so in the habit of going that I couldn't stay away. After one or two Sabbaths, back again to the house of God I went. There I first found Christ, and I have often said since,

"Mother, I thank you for making me go to the house of God when I didn't want to go."

Parents, if you want your children to grow up and honor you, have them honor the Sabbath day. Don't let them go off fishing and getting into bad company, or it won't be long before they will come home and curse you. I know few things more beautiful than to see a father and mother coming up the aisle with their daughters and sons, and sitting down together to hear the Word of God. It is a good thing to have the children, not in some remote loft or gallery, but in a good place, well in sight. Though they cannot understand the sermon now, when they get older they won't desire to break away, they will continue attending public worship in the house of God.

But we must not mistake the means for the end. We must not think that the Sabbath is just for the sake of being able to attend meetings. There are some people who think they must spend the whole day at meetings or private devotions. The result is that at nightfall they are tired out, and the day has brought them no rest. The number of church services attended ought to be measured by the person's ability to enjoy them and get good from them, without being wearied. Attending meetings is not the only way to observe the Sabbath. The Israelites were commanded to keep it in their dwellings as well as in holy convocation. The home, that center of so great influence over the life and character of the people, ought to be made the scene of true Sabbath observance.

HOME OBSERVANCE

Jeremiah classified godless families with the heathen: "Pour out thy fury upon the heathen that know thee not, and upon the families that call not on thy name: for they have eaten up Jacob, devoured him, and consumed him, and have made his habitation desolate" (10:25).

Many mothers have written to me at one time or another to know what to do to entertain their children on the Sabbath. The boys say, "I do wish 'twas night," or, "I do hate the Sabbath," or, "I do wish the Sabbath were over." It ought to be the happiest day in the week to them, one to be looked forward to with pleasure. In order to this end, many suggestions might be followed. Make family prayers especially attractive by having the children learn some verse or story from the Bible. Give more time to your children than you can give on weekdays, reading to them and perhaps taking them to walk in the afternoon or evening. Show by your conduct that the Sabbath is a delight, and they will soon catch your spirit. Set aside some time for religious instruction, without making this a task. You can make it interesting for the children by telling Bible stories and asking them to guess the names of the characters. Have Sunday games for the younger children. Picture books, puzzle maps of Palestine, and such things can be easily obtained. Sunday albums and Sunday clocks are other devices. Set aside attractive books for the Sabbath, not letting the children have these during the week. By doing this, the children can be brought to look forward to the day with eagerness and pleasure.

PRIVATE OBSERVANCE

Apart from public and family observance, the individual ought to devote a portion of the time to his own edification. Prayer, meditation, reading, ought not to be forgotten. Think of men devoting six days a week to their body, which will soon pass away, and begrudging one day to the soul, which will live on and on forever! Is it too much for God to ask for one day to be devoted to the growth and training of the spiritual senses, when the other senses are kept busy the other six days?

If your circumstances permit, engage in some definite Christian work, such as teaching in Sunday school, or visiting the sick. Do all the good you can. Sin keeps no Sabbath, and no more should good deeds. There is plenty of opportunity in this fallen world to perform works of mercy and religion. Make your Sabbath down here a foretaste of the eternal Sabbath that is in store for believers.

You want power in your Christian life, do you? You want Holy Ghost power? You want the dew of heaven on your brow? You want to see men convicted and converted? I don't believe we shall ever have genuine conversions until we get straight on this law of God.

Sabbath Desecration

Men seem to think they have a right to change the holy day into a *holiday*. The young have more temptations to break the Sabbath than we had forty years ago. There are three great temptations: first the trolley car, that will take you off into the country for a nickel to have a day of recreation; second, the bicycle, which is leading a good many Christian men to give up their Sabbath and spend the day on excursions; and the third, the Sunday newspaper.

Twenty years ago Christian people in Chicago would have been horrified if anyone had prophesied that all the theaters would be open every Sabbath; but that is what has come to pass. If it had been prophesied twenty years ago that Christian men would take a wheel and go off on Sunday morning and be gone all day on an excursion, Christians would have been horrified and would have said it was impossible; but that is what is going on today all over the country.

THE SUNDAY NEWSPAPER

With regard to the Sunday newspaper, I know all the arguments that are brought in its favor—that the work on it is done during the week, that it is the Monday paper that causes Sunday work, and so on. But there are two hundred thousand newsboys selling the paper on Sunday. Would you like to have your boy one of them? Men are kept running trains in order to distribute the papers. Would you like your Sabbath taken away from you? If not, then practice the Golden Rule, and don't touch the papers.

Their contents make them unfit for reading any day, not to say Sunday. Some New York dailies advertise Sunday editions of sixty pages. Many dirty pieces of scandal in this and other countries are raked up and put into them. "Eight pages of fun!"— that is splendid reading for Sunday, isn't it? Even when a so-called sermon is printed, it is completely buried by the fiction and news matter. It is time that ministers went into their pulpits and preached against Sunday newspapers if they haven't done it already.

Put the man in the scales that buys and reads Sunday papers. After reading them for two or three hours he might go and hear the best sermon in the world, but you couldn't preach anything into him.

His mind is filled up with what he has read, and there is no room for thoughts of God. I believe that the archangel Gabriel himself could not make an impression on an audience that has its head full of such trash. If you bored a hole into a man's head, you could not inject any thoughts of God and heaven.

I don't believe that the publishers would allow their own children to read them. Why then should they give them to my children and to yours?

A merchant who advertises in Sunday papers is not keeping the Sabbath. It is a master-stroke of the devil to induce Christian men to do this in order to make trade for Monday. But if a man makes money, and yet his sons are ruined and his home broken up, what has he gained?

Ladies buy the Sunday papers and read the advertisements of Monday bargains to see what they can buy cheap. Just so with their religion. They are willing to have it if it doesn't cost anything. If Christian men and women refused to buy them, if Christian merchants refused to advertise in them, they would soon die out, because that is where they get most of their support.

They tell me the Sunday paper has come to stay, and I may as well let it alone. Never! I believe it is a great evil, and I shall fight it while I live. I never read a Sunday paper, and wouldn't have one in my house. They are often sent me, but I tear them up without reading them. I will have nothing to do with them. They do more harm to religion than any other one agency I know. Their whole influence is against keeping the Sabbath holy. They are an unnecessary evil. Can't a man read enough news on weekdays without desecrating the Sabbath? We had no Sunday papers till the war came, and we got along very well without them. They have been increasing in size and in number ever since then, and I think they have been lowering their tone ever since. If you believe that, help to fight them too. Stamp them out, beginning with yourself.

PUNISHMENT OR BLESSING?

No nation has ever prospered that has trampled the Sabbath in the dust. Show me a nation that has done this and I will show you a nation that has got in it the seeds of ruin and decay. I believe that Sabbath desecration will carry a nation down quicker than anything else. Adam brought marriage and the Sabbath with him out of Eden, and neither can be disregarded without suffering. When the children of Israel went into the Promised Land, God told them to let their land rest every seven years, and He would give them as much in six years as in seven. For four hundred and ninety years they disregarded that law. But mark you, Nebuchadnezzar came and took them off into Babylon, and kept them seventy years in captivity, and the land had its seventy sabbaths of rest. Seven times seventy is four hundred and ninety. So they did not gain much by breaking this law. You can give God His day, or He will take it.

On the other hand, honoring the fourth commandment brings blessing: "If thou turn away thy foot from the sabbath, from doing thy pleasure on my holy day; and call the sabbath a delight, the holy of the LORD, honorable; and shalt honor him, not doing thine own ways, nor finding thine own pleasure,

nor speaking thine own words ['thine own' as con-
trasted with what God enjoins]: then shalt thou delight thyself in the LORD; and I will cause thee to ride
upon the high places of the earth, and feed thee with
the heritage of Jacob thy father, for the mouth of the
LORD hath spoken it" (Is 58:13-14).

I do not know what will become of this republic if
we give up our Christian Sabbath. If Satan can break
the conscience down on one point, he can break it
down on all. When I was in France in 1867, I could
not tell one day from the other. On Sunday, stores
were open and buildings were erected, the same as on
other days. See how quickly that country went down.
One hundred years ago France and England stood
abreast in the march of nations. Where do they
stand today? France undertook to wipe out the Sabbath, and has pretty nearly wiped itself out, while
England belts the globe.

A FIRM STAND

We have a fighting chance to save this nation, and
what we want is men and women who have moral
courage to stand up and say:

"No, I will not touch the Sunday paper, and all the
influence I have I will throw dead against it. I will
not go away on Saturday evening if I have to travel
on Sunday to get back. I will not do unnecessary
work on the Sabbath. I will do all I can to keep it
holy as God commanded."

But someone says: "Mr. Moody, what are you going to do? I have to work seven days a week or
starve."

Then starve! Wouldn't it be a grand thing to have

a martyr in the nineteenth century? "The blood of the martyrs is the seed of the church." Someone says the seed is getting very low; it has been a long time since we have had any seed. I would give something to erect a monument to such a martyr for his fidelity to God's law. I would go around the world to attend his funeral.

We want today men who will make up their minds to do what is right and stand by it if the heavens tumble on their heads. What is to become of Christian Associations and Sunday schools, of churches and Christian Endeavor societies, if the Christian Sabbath is given up to recreation and made a holiday? Hasn't the time come to call a halt if men want power with God? Let men call you narrow and bigoted, but be man enough to stand by God's law, and you will have power and blessing. That is the kind of Christianity we want just now in this country. Any man can go with the crowd, but we want men who will go against the current.

Sabbath-breaker, are you ready to step into the scales?

PUBLISHER'S NOTE

The author of this book was not an
advocate of the tenets of
Seventh Day Adventism.

The Fifth Commandment

Honour thy father and thy mother: that thy days may be long upon the land which the LORD *thy God giveth thee.*

WE ARE LIVING in dark days on this question too. It really seems as if the days the apostle Paul wrote about are upon us: "In the last days perilous times shall come. For men shall be lovers of their own selves, covetous, boasters, proud, blasphemers, disobedient to parents, unthankful, unholy, without natural affection, . . . despisers of those that are good" (2 Ti 3:1-3). If Paul were alive today, could he have described the present state of affairs more truly? There are perhaps more men in this country that are breaking the hearts of their fathers and mothers and trampling on the law of God than in any other civilized country in the world. How many sons treat their parents with contempt and make light of their entreaties? A young man will have the kindest care from parents; they will watch over him and care for all his wants, and some bad companion will come in and sweep him away from them in a few weeks. How many young ladies have married against their parents' wishes and have gone off and made their own life bitter! I never knew one case that did not turn out badly. They invariably bring ruin upon themselves unless they repent.

BEGIN IN THE HOME

The first four commandments deal with our relations to God. They tell us how to worship and when to worship; they forbid irreverence and impiety in word and act. Now God turns to our relations with each other, and isn't it significant that He deals first with family life? "God is going to show us our duty to our neighbor. How does He begin? Not by telling us how kings ought to reign, or how soldiers ought to fight, or how merchants ought to conduct their business, but how boys and girls ought to behave at home."

We can see that if their home life is all right, they are almost sure to fulfill the law in regard to both God and man. Parents stand in the place of God to their children in a great many ways until the children arrive at years of discretion. If the children are true to their parents, it will be easier for them to be true to God. He used the human relationship as a symbol of our relationship to Him both by creation and by grace. God is our Father in heaven. We are His offspring.

On the other hand, if they have not learned to be obedient and respectful at home, they are likely to have little respect for the law of the land. It is all in the heart; and the heart is prepared at home for good or bad conduct outside. The tree grows the way the twig is bent.

"Honour thy father and thy mother." That word *honor* means more than mere obedience—a child may obey through fear. It means love and affection, gratitude, respect. We are told that in the East the words "father" and "mother" include those who are "superiors in age, wisdom and in civil or religious station," so that when the Jews were taught to honor their father and mother it included all who were placed over them in these relations, as well as their parents. Isn't there a crying need for that same feeling today? The lawlessness of the present time is a natural consequence of the growing absence of a feeling of respect for those in authority.

HONOR THY MOTHER

It has been pointed out as worthy of notice that this commandment enjoins honor for *the mother,* and yet in eastern countries the present-day woman is held of little account. When I was in Palestine a few years ago, the prettiest girl in Jericho was sold by her father in exchange for a donkey. In many ancient nations, just as in certain parts of heathendom today, the parents are killed off as soon as they become old and feeble. Can't we see the hand of God here, raising the woman to her rightful position of honor out of the degradation into which she had been dragged by heathenism?

"Honour thy father and thy mother: that thy days may be long upon the land which the LORD thy God giveth thee." I believe that we must get back to the old truths. You may make light of it and laugh at it, young man, but remember that God has given this commandment, and you cannot set it aside. If we get back to this law, we shall have power and blessing.

TEMPORAL BLESSING OR CURSE

I believe it to be literally true that our temporal condition depends on the way we act upon this commandment. "Honour thy father and mother, (which is the first commandment with promise), that it may be well with thee, and that thou mayest live long on the earth." "Honour thy father and thy mother, as the Lord thy God hath commanded thee; that thy days may be prolonged, and that it may go well with thee, in the land which the Lord thy God giveth thee." "Cursed is he that setteth light by his father or mother." "Whoso curseth his father or mother, his lamp shall be put out in obscure darkness."

It would be easy to multiply texts from the Bible to prove this truth. Experience teaches the same thing. A good, loving son generally turns out better than a refractory son. Obedience and respect at home prepare the way for obedience to the employer, and are joined with other virtues that help toward a prosperous career, crowned with a ripe, honored old age. Disobedience and disrespect for parents are often the first steps in the downward track. Many a criminal has testified that this is the point where he first went astray. I have lived over sixty years, and I have learned one thing if I have learned nothing else—that no man or woman who dishonors father or mother ever prospers.

Young man, young woman, how do you treat your parents? Tell me that, and I will tell you how you are going to get on in life. When I hear a young man speaking contemptuously of his grey-haired father or mother, I say he has sunk very low indeed. When

I see a young man as polite as any gentleman can be when he is out in society, but who snaps at his mother and speaks unkindly to his father, I would not give the snap of my finger for his religion. If there is any man or woman on earth that ought to be treated kindly and tenderly, it is that loving mother or that loving father. If they cannot have your regard through life, what reward are they to have for all their care and anxiety? Think how they loved you and provided for you in your early days.

A Mother's Love

Let your mind go back to the time when you were ill. Did your mother neglect you? When a neighbor came in and said, "Now, mother, you go and lie down; you have been up for a week; I will take your place for a night"—did she do it? No; and if the poor worn body forced her to it at last, she lay watching, and if she heard your voice, she was at your side directly, anticipating all your wants, wiping the perspiration away from your brow. If you wanted water, how soon you got it! She would gladly have taken the disease into her own body to save you. Her love for you would drive her to any lengths. No matter to what depths of vice and misery you have sunk, no matter how profligate you have grown, she has not turned you out of her heart. Perhaps she loves you all the more because you are wayward. She would draw you back by the bands of a love that never dies.

Filial Ingratitude

When I was in England, I read of a man who professed to be a Christian, who was brought before the magistrate for not supporting his aged father. He had let him go to the workhouse. My friends, I'd rather be content with a crust of bread and a drink of water than let my father or mother go to the workhouse. The idea of a professing Christian doing such a thing! God have mercy on such a godless Christianity as that! It is a withered-up thing, and the breath of heaven will drive it away. Don't profess to love God and do a thing like that.

A friend of mine told me of a poor man who had sent his son to school in the city. One day the father was hauling some wood into the city, perhaps to pay his boy's bills. The young man was walking down the street with two of his school friends, all dressed in the very height of fashion. His father saw him, and was so glad that he left his wood, and went to the sidewalk to speak to him. But the boy was ashamed of his father, who had on his old working clothes, and spurned him, and said:

"I don't know you."

Will such a young man ever amount to anything? Never!

I remember a very promising young man whom I had in the Sunday school in Chicago. His father was a confirmed drunkard, and his mother took in washing to educate her four children. This was her eldest son, and I thought that he was going to redeem the whole family. But one day a thing happened that made him go down in my estimation.

The boy was in the high school, and was a very bright scholar. One day he stood with his mother at the cottage door—it was a poor house, but she could not pay for their schooling, and feed and clothe her children, and hire a very good house too, out of her earnings. When they were talking a young man from the high school came up the street, and this boy walked away from his mother. Next day the young man said:

"Who was that I saw you talking to yesterday?"

"Oh, that was my washerwoman."

I said: "Poor fellow! He will never amount to anything."

That was a good many years ago. I have kept my eye on him. He has gone down, down, down, and now he is just a miserable wreck. Of course he would go down. Ashamed of his mother who loved him and toiled for him, and bore so much hardship for him! I cannot tell you the contempt I had for that one act.

Let us look at

A BRIGHTER PICTURE

Some years ago I heard of a poor woman who sent her boy to school and college. When he was to graduate, he wrote his mother to come, but she sent back word that she could not because her only skirt had already been turned once. She was so shabby that she was afraid he would be ashamed of her. He wrote back that he didn't care how she was dressed and urged so strongly that she went. He met her at the station, and took her to a nice place to stay. The day came for his graduation, and he walked down the broad aisle with that poor mother dressed very shabbily, and put her into one of the best seats in the house. To her great surprise he was the valedictorian of the class, and he carried everything before him.

He won a prize, and when it was given to him, he stepped down before the whole audience, and kissed his mother, and said:

"Here, mother, here is the prize. It is yours. I would not have had it if it had not been for you."

Thank God for such a man!

The one glimpse the Bible gives us of thirty out of the thirty-three years of Christ's life on earth shows that He did not come to destroy this fifth commandment. The secret of all those silent years is embodied in that verse in Luke's Gospel—"And he went down with them and came to Nazareth, and was subject to them." Did He not set an example of true filial love and care when in the midst of the agonies of the cross He made provision for His mother? Did He not condemn the miserable evasions of this law by the Pharisees of His own day:

"Well hath Esaias prophesied of you hypocrites, as it is written, This people honoureth me with their lips, but their heart is far from me. Howbeit in vain do they worship me, teaching for doctrines the commandments of men. . . . Full well do ye reject the commandment of God, that ye may keep your own tradition. For Moses said, Honour thy father and thy mother; and, Whoso curseth father or mother, let him die the death: but ye say, If a man shall say to his father or mother, It is Corban, that is to say, a gift, by whatsoever thou mightest be profited by me; he shall be free. And ye suffer him no more to do ought for his father or his mother; making the word of God of none effect by your tradition, which ye have delivered" (Mk 7:6-13).

I have read of one heathen custom in China, which

would do us credit in this so-called Christian country. On every New Year's morning each man and boy, from the emperor to the lowest peasant, is said to pay a visit to his mother, carrying her a present varying in value according to his station in life. He thanks her for all she has done for him and asks a continuance of her favor another year. Abraham Lincoln used to say: "All I have I owe to my mother."

I would rather die a hundred deaths than have my children grow up to treat me with scorn and contempt. I would rather have them honor me a thousand times over than have the world honor me. I would rather have their esteem and favor than the esteem of the whole world. And any man who seeks the honor and esteem of the world, and doesn't treat his parents right, is sure to be disappointed.

An Exhortation

Young man, if your parents are still living, treat them kindly. Do all you can to make their declining years sweet and happy. Bear in mind that this is the only commandment that you may not always be able to obey. As long as you live, you will be able to serve God, to keep the sabbath, to obey all the other commandments; but the day comes to most men when father and mother die. What bitter feelings you will have when the opportunity has gone by if you fail to show them the respect and love that is their due! How long is it since you wrote to your mother? Perhaps you have not written home for months, or it may be for years. How often I get letters from mothers urging me to try to influence their sons!

Which would you rather be—a Joseph or an Absalom? Joseph wasn't satisfied until he had brought his old father down into Egypt. He was the greatest man in Egypt, next to Pharaoh; he was arrayed in the finest garments; he had Pharaoh's ring on his hand, and a gold chain about his neck, and they cried before him, "Bow the knee." Yet when he heard Jacob was coming, he hurried out to meet him. He wasn't ashamed of the old man with his shepherd's clothes. What a contrast we see in Absalom. That young man broke his father's heart by his rebellion, and the Jews are said to throw a stone at Absalom's pillar to the present day, whenever they pass it, as a token of their horror of Absalom's unnatural conduct.

Come, now, are you ready to be weighed? If you have been dishonoring your father and mother, step into the scales and see how quickly you will be found wanting. See how quickly you will strike the beam. I don't know any man who is much lighter than one who treats his parents with contempt. Do you disobey them just as much as you dare? Do you try to deceive them? Do you call them old-fashioned, and sneer at their advice? How do you treat that venerable father and praying mother?

You may be a professing Christian, but I wouldn't give much for your religion unless it gets into your life and teaches you how to live. I wouldn't give a snap of my finger for a religion that doesn't begin at home and regulate your conduct—toward your parents.

The Sixth Commandment

Thou shalt not kill.

I USED TO SAY: "What is the use of taking up a law like this in an audience where, probably, there isn't a man who ever thought of, or ever will commit, murder?" But as one gets on in years, he sees many a murder that is not outright killing. I need not kill a person to be a murderer. If I get so angry that I wish a man dead, I am a murderer in God's sight. God looks at the heart and says he that hateth his brother is a murderer.

First, let us see what this commandment does not mean.

It does not forbid the killing of animals for food and for other reasons. Millions of rams and lambs and turtle-doves must have been killed every year for sacrifices under the Mosaic system. Christ Himself ate of the Passover lamb, and we are told definitely of cases where He ate fish and provided it for His disciples and the people to eat.

It does not forbid the killing of burglars or attackers in self-defense. Directly after the giving of the Ten Commandments, God laid down the ordinance that if a thief be found breaking in and be smitten that he die, it was pardonable. Did not Christ justify this idea of self-defense when He said: "If the good-man of the house had known in what watch the thief would come, he would have watched, and would not have suffered his house to be broken up" (Mt 24:43).

It does not forbid capital punishment. God Him-self set the death penalty upon violations of each of the first seven commandments, as well as for other crimes. God said to Noah after the deluge, "Whoso sheddeth man's blood, by man shall his blood be shed" (Gen 9:2); and the reason given is just as true today as it was then—"for in the image of God made he man."

What it does forbid is the wanton, intentional tak-ing of human life under wrong motives and circum-stances. Man is made in God's image. He is built for eternity. He is more than a mere animal. His life ought therefore to be held sacred. Once taken, it can never be restored. In heathen lands human life is no more sacred than the life of animals; even in Christian lands there are heartless and selfish men who hold it cheap; but God has invested it with a high value. An infidel philosopher of the eighteenth century said: "In the sight of God, every event is alike important; and the life of a man is of no greater importance to the universe than that of an oyster." "Where is the crime," he asked, "of turning a few ounces of blood out of their channel?" Such lan-guage needs no answer.

THE VALUE OF MAN

Let me give you a passage from H. L. Hastings: "A friend of mine visited the Fiji Islands in 1844, and what do you suppose an infidel was worth there then? You could buy a man for a musket, or if you paid money, for seven dollars, and after you had bought him you could feed him, starve him, work him, whip him, or eat him—they generally ate them, unless they were so full of tobacco they could not stomach them! But if you go there today you could not buy a man for seven million dollars. There are no men for sale there now. What has made the difference in the price of humanity? The twelve hundred Christian chapels scattered over that island tell the story. The people have learned to read that Book which says: 'Ye were not redeemed with corruptible things, as silver and gold, . . . but with the precious blood of Christ' (1 Pe 1:18-19); and since they learned that lesson, no man is for sale there."

Men tell me that the world is getting so much better. We talk of our American civilization. We forget the alarming increase of crime in our midst. It is said that there is no civilized country on the globe where murder is so frequently committed and so seldom punished.

SUICIDE

There is that other kind of murder that is increasing at an appalling rate among us—suicide. There have been infidels in all ages who have advocated it as a justifiable means of release from trial and difficulty; yet thinking men, as far back as Aristotle, have generally condemned it as cowardly and unjustifiable under any conditions. No man has a right to take his own life from such motives any more than the life of another.

It has been pointed out that the Jewish race, the

people of God, always counted length of days as a blessing. The Bible does not mention one single instance of a good man committing suicide. In the four thousand years of Old Testament history it records only four suicides, and only one suicide in the New Testament. Saul, king of Israel, and his armorbearer, Ahithophel, Zimri and Judas Iscariot are the five cases. Look at the references in the Bible to see what kind of men they were.

OTHER KINDS OF MURDER

But I want to speak of other classes of murderers that are very numerous in this country, although they are not classified as murderers. The man who is the cause of the death of another through criminal carelessness is guilty. The man who sells diseased meat; the saloon-keeper whose drink has maddened the brain of a criminal; those who adulterate food; the employer who jeopardizes the lives of employees and others by unsafe surroundings and conditions in harmful occupations—they are all guilty of blood where life is lost as a consequence.

When I was in England in 1892, I met a gentleman who claimed that they were ahead of us in the respect they had for the law. "We hang our murderers," he said, "but there isn't one out of twenty in your country that is hung." I said, "You are greatly mistaken, for they walk about these two countries unhung." "What do you mean?" "I will tell you what I mean," I said; "the man that comes into my house and runs a dagger into my heart for my money, is a prince compared with a son that takes five years to kill me and the wife of my bosom. A young man who comes home night after night drunk, and when his mother remonstrates, curses her grey hairs and kills her by inches, is the blackest kind of a murderer."

That kind of thing is going on constantly all around us. One young man at college, an only son, whose mother wrote to him remonstrating against his gambling and drinking habits, took the letters out of the post-office, and when he found that they were from her, he tore them up without reading them. She said, "I thought I would die when I found I had lost my hold on that son."

If a boy kills his mother by his conduct, you can't call it anything else than *murder,* and he is as truly guilty of breaking this sixth commandment as if he drove a dagger to her heart. If all young men in this country who are killing their parents and their wives by inches, should be hung this next week, there would be a great many funerals.

How are you treating your parents? Come, are you killing them? This sixth commandment follows very naturally after the fifth, "Honor thy father and thy mother." Don't put any thorns in their pillows and make their last days miserable. Bear in mind that the commandment refers not only to shooting a man down in cold blood; but he is the worst murderer who goes on, month after month, year after year, until he has crowded the life out of a sainted mother and put a godly father under the sod.

THE WORDS OF CHRIST

Let us look once again at the Sermon on the Mount, that men think so much of, and see what

Christ had to say: "Ye have heard that it was said by them of old time, Thou shalt not kill; and whosoever shall kill shall be in danger of the judgment: but I say unto you, That whosoever is angry with his brother without a cause shall be in danger of the judgment: and whosoever shall say to his brother, Raca [an expression of contempt], shall be in danger of the council: but whosoever shall say, Thou fool [an expression of condemnation], shall be in danger of hell fire (Mt 5:21-22). "Three degrees of murderous guilt," as has been said, "all of which can be manifested without a blow being struck: secret anger; the spiteful jeer; the open, unrestrained outburst of violent, abusive speech."

Again, what does John say? "Whosoever hateth his brother is a murderer: and ye know that no murderer hath eternal life abiding in him" (1 Jn 3:15).

Did you ever in your heart wish a man dead? That was murder. Did you ever get so angry that you wished any one harm? Then you are guilty. I may be addressing someone who is cultivating an unforgiving spirit. That is the spirit of the murderer, and needs to be rooted out of your heart.

We can only read men's acts—what they have done. God looks down into the heart. That is the birthplace and home of the evil desires and intentions that lead to the transgression of all God's laws.

Listen once more to the words of Jesus: "From within, out of the heart of men, proceed evil thoughts, adulteries, fornications, murders, thefts, covetousness, wickedness, deceit, lasciviousness, an evil eye, blasphemy, pride, foolishness" (Mk 7:21-22).

May God purge our hearts of these evil things, if we are harboring them! Ah, if many of us were weighed now, we should find Belshazzar's doom written against us—"Tekel—wanting!"

The Seventh Commandment

Thou shalt not commit adultery.

AN ENGLISH ARMY-OFFICER in India who had been living an impure life went around one evening to argue religion with the chaplain. During their talk the officer said:

"Religion is all very well, but you must admit that there are difficulties—about the miracles, for instance."

The chaplain knew the man and his besetting sin, and quietly looking him in the face, answered:

"Yes, there are some things in the Bible not very plain, I admit: but the seventh commandment is very plain."

PLAIN SPEAKING

I would to God I could pass over this commandment, but I feel that the time has come to cry aloud and spare not. Plain speaking about it is not very fashionable nowadays. "Teachers of religion have by common consent banished from their public teaching all advice, warning or allusion in regard to love between the sexes," says Dr. Stalker. These themes are left to poets and novelists to handle. In an autobiography recently published in England, the writer attributed no small share of the follies and vices of his earlier years to his never having heard a plain, outspoken sermon on this seventh commandment.

But though men are inclined to pass it by, God is not silent or indifferent in regard to it. When I hear anyone make light of adultery and licentiousness, I take the Bible and see how God has let His curse and wrath come down upon it.

"Thou shalt not commit adultery" (Ex 20:14); "For this is a heinous crime; yea, it is an iniquity to be punished by the judges. For it is a fire that consumeth to destruction, and would root out all mine increase" (Job 31:11-12); "By means of a whorish woman a man is brought to a piece of bread: and the adulteress will hunt for the precious life. Can a man take fire in his bosom, and his clothes not be burned? Can one go upon hot coals, and his feet not be burned? So he that goeth in to his neighbor's wife; whosoever toucheth her shall not be innocent" (Pr 6: 26:28); "Whoso committeth adultery with a woman lacketh understanding: he that doeth it destroyeth his own soul. A wound and dishonor shall he get; and his reproach shall not be wiped away" (Pr 6:32-33).

"Know ye not that the unrighteous shall not inherit the kingdom of God? Be not deceived: neither fornicators, . . . nor adulterers, nor effeminate, nor abusers of themselves with mankind . . . shall inherit the kingdom of God" (1 Co 6:9-10); "But fornication, and all uncleanness, . . . let it not be once named among you, as becometh saints; neither filthiness, nor foolish talking, nor jesting, which are not convenient: but rather giving of thanks. For this ye know, that no whoremonger, nor unclean person . . . hath any inheritance in the kingdom of Christ and of God. Let no man deceive you with vain words: for because of these things cometh the wrath of God upon the children of disobedience. Be not ye therefore partakers with them" (Eph 5:5-6); "Whoremongers . . . shall have their part in the lake which burneth with fire and brimstone: which is the second death" (Rev 21:8).

These are a few of the threatenings and warnings contained in the old Book, up to its closing chapter. It speaks plainly, without compromise.

MARRIAGE AND THE HOME

This commandment is God's bulwark around marriage and the home. Marriage is one of the institutions that existed in Eden; it is older than the Fall. It is the most sacred relationship that can exist between human beings, taking precedence even of the relationship of the parent and child. Someone has pointed out that as in the beginning God created one man and one woman, this is the true order for all ages. Where family ties are disregarded and dishonored, the results are always fatal. The home existed before the Church, and unless the home is kept pure and undefiled, there can be no family religion, and the church is in danger.

Adultery and licentiousness have swept nation after nation out of existence. Did it not bring fire and brimstone from heaven upon Sodom and Gomorrah? What carried Rome into ruin? The obscene frescoes and statues at Pompeii and Naples tell the tale.

Where there is no sacredness around the home, population dwindles; family virtues disappear; the children are corrupt from their very birth; the seeds of sure decay are already planted. In 1895 there were twenty-five thousand divorces in this country. I was on one of the fashionable streets of a prominent city some time ago, where every family except two in the whole street had either a son or a daughter that had been divorced. Divorce and debauchery go hand in hand. We are not gaining much in turning away from this old law, are we?

THE DEVIL'S COUNTERFEIT

Lust is the devil's counterfeit of love. There is nothing more beautiful on earth than a pure love, and there is nothing so blighting as lust. I do not know of a quicker, shorter way down to hell than by adultery and the kindred sins condemned by this commandment. The Bible says that with the heart man believeth unto righteousness, but "whoredom and wine and new wine take away the heart" (Ho 4: 11). Lust will drive all natural affection out of a man's heart. For the sake of some vile harlot he will trample on the feelings and entreaties of a sainted mother and beautiful wife and godly sister.

Young man, are you leading an impure life? Suppose God's scales should drop down before you, what would you do? Are you fit for the kingdom of heaven? You know very well that you are not. You loathe yourself. When you look upon that pure wife or mother, you say,

"What a vile wretch I am! The harlot is bringing me down to an untimely and dishonored grave."

May God show us what a fearful sin it is! The idea of making light of it! I do not know of any sin that will make a man run down to ruin more quickly. I am appalled when I think of what is going on in the world; of so many young men living impure lives, and talking about the virtue of women as if it didn't amount to anything. This sin is coming in upon us like a flood at the present day. In every city there is an army of prostitutes. Young men by hundreds are being utterly ruined by this accursed sin.

The Prodigal Daughter

I think that the most infernal thing that shines on in America is the way a woman is treated after she has been ruined by a man, often under fair promises of marriage. Someone said that when the prodigal son came home he had the best robe and the fatted calf, but what does the prodigal daughter get? Although she may have been more sinned against than sinning, she is cast out and ostracized by society. She is condemned to an almost hopeless life of degradation and shame, sinking step by step into a loathsome grave, unless she hurries her doom by suicide. But the wretch who has ruined her in body and soul holds his head as high as ever, and society attaches no stain to him. If he had failed to pay his gambling debts, or was detected cheating at cards, he would promptly be dropped by society; but he may boast of his impure life, and his companions will think nothing of it. Parents who would not allow their daughters to become acquainted with a man who is rude in manners, sometimes do not hesitate to accept the society of men who are known to be impure.

Talk about stealing—a man who steals the virtue of a woman is the meanest thief that ever was on the face of the earth! One who goes into your house and steals your money is a prince compared with a vile libertine who takes the virtue of your sister, or steals the affection of your wife, and robs you of her; no sneak thief that ever walked the earth is so mean as he. How men pass laws to protect their property, but when that which is far nearer and dearer to them than money is taken, it is made light of! If a man should push a young lady into the river and she should be drowned, the law would lay hold of him, and he would be tried for murder and hung. But if he wins her affection and ruins her, and then casts her off, isn't he worse than a murderer? There are some sins that are worse than murder, and that is one of them. If someone should treat your wife or sister so, you would want to shoot him as you would a dog. Why do you not respect all women as you do your mother and sister? What law of justice forgives the obscene bird of prey, while it kicks out of its path the soiled and bleeding dove?

God's Coming Judgment

God has appointed a day when this matter will be set right. "Be not deceived; God is not mocked: whatsoever a man soweth, that shall he also reap" (Gal 6:7). He will render to every man according to his deeds. You may walk down the aisle of the church and take your seat, thinking that no one knows of your sin. But God is on the throne, and He will surely bring you to judgment. Do you believe that God will allow this infernal thing to go on—women bearing all the blame while guilty men go unpunished? God has appointed a day when He will judge this world in righteousness, and the day is fast approaching.

If you are guilty of this sin, do not let the day pass until you repent. If you are living in some secret sin or are fostering impure thoughts, make up your mind that by the grace of God you will be delivered. I don't believe a man who is guilty of this sin is ever going to see the kingdom of God unless he repents in sackcloth and ashes, and does all he can to make restitution.

AN EVIL HARVEST

Even in this life adultery and uncleanness bring their awful results, both physical and mental. The pleasure and excitement that lead so many astray at the beginning soon pass away, and only the evil remains. Vice carries a sting in its tail, like the scorpion. The body is sinned against, and the body sooner or later suffers. "Every sin that a man doeth is without the body; but he that committeth fornication sinneth against his own body" (1 Co 6:18), said Paul. Nature herself punishes with nameless diseases, and the man goes down to the grave rotten, leaving the effects of his sin to blight his posterity. There are nations whose manhood has been eaten out by this awful scourge.

It drags a man lower than the beasts. It stains the memory. I believe that memory is "the worm that never dies," and the memory is never cleansed of ob-

scene stories and unclean acts. Even if a man repents and reforms he often has to fight the past.

Lust gave Samson into the power of Delilah, who
robbed him of his strength. It led David to commit
murder and called down upon him the wrath of God,
and if he had not repented he would have lost heaven.
I believe that if Joseph had responded to the entice-
ment of Potiphar's wife, his light would have gone
out in darkness.

It ends in one or other of two ways: either in re-
morse and shame because of the realization of the
loss of purity, with a terrible struggle against a hard
taskmaster; or in hardness of heart, brutalizing of the
finer senses, which is a more dreadful condition.

We hear a good deal about intemperance nowadays. That sin advertises itself; it shows its marks
upon the face and in the conduct. But this hides itself away under the shadow of the night. A man who
tampers with this evil goes on step by step until his
character is blasted, his reputation ruined, his health
gone, and his life made as dark as hell. May God
wake up the nation to see how this awful sin is
spreading!

Will anyone deny that the house of the strange
woman is "the way to hell, going down to the cham-
bers of death," as the Bible says? Are there not men
whose characters have been utterly ruined for this
life through this accursed sin? Are there not wives
who would rather sink into their graves than live?
Many a man went with a pure woman to the altar a
few years ago and promised to love and cherish her.
Now he has given his affections to some vile harlot
and brought ruin on his wife and children!

ARE YOU GUILTY?

Young man, young woman, are you guilty, even in thought? Bear in mind what Christ said: "Ye have heard that it was said by them of old time, Thou shalt not commit adultery: but I say unto you, That whosoever looketh on a woman to lust after her has committed adultery with her already in his heart" (Mt 5: 27-28). How many would repent but that they are tied hand and foot, and some vile harlot whose feet are fastened in hell, clings to him and says: "If you give me up, I will expose you!" Can you step on the scales and take that harlot with you?

If you are guilty of this awful sin, escape for your life. Hear God's voice while there is yet time. Confess your sin to Him. Ask Him to snap the fetters that bind you. Ask Him to give you victory over your passions. If your right eye offends, pluck it out. If your right hand offends, cut it off. Shake yourself like Samson, and say:

"By the grace of God I will not go down to an adulterer's grave."

There is hope for you, adulterer. There is hope for you, adulteress. God will not turn you away if you truly repent. No matter how low down in vice and misery you may have sunk, you may be washed, you may be sanctified, you may be justified in the name of the Lord Jesus, and by the Spirit of our God. Remember what Christ said to that woman which was a sinner, "Thy sins are forgiven . . . thy faith hath saved thee; go in peace" (Lk 7:47); and to that woman that was taken in adultery, "Go, and sin no more" (Jn 8:11).

The Eighth Commandment

Thou shalt not steal.

DURING THE TIME of slavery, a slave was preaching with great power. His master heard of it, and sent for him, and said:

"I understand you are preaching?"

"Yes," said the slave.

"Well, now," said the master, "I will give you all the time you need, and I want you to prepare a sermon on the Ten Commandments, and to bear down especially on stealing, because there is a great deal of stealing on the plantation."

The slave's countenance fell at once. He said he wouldn't like to do that; there wasn't the warmth in that subject there was in others.

I have noticed that people are satisfied when you preach about the sins of the patriarchs, but they don't like it when you touch upon the sins of today. That is coming too near home. But we need to have these old doctrines stated over and over again in our churches. Perhaps it is not necessary to speak here about the grosser violations of this eighth commandment, because the law of the land looks after these; but a man or woman can steal without cracking safes and picking pockets. Many a person who would shrink from taking what belongs to another person thinks nothing of stealing from the government or from large public corporations, such as street car companies. If you steal from a rich man it is as much a sin as stealing from a poor man. If you lie about the value of things you buy, are you not trying to defraud the storekeeper? "It is naught, it is naught, saith the buyer: but when he is gone his way, then he boasteth" (Pr 20:14).

On the other hand, many a person who would not steal himself, holds stock in companies that make dishonest profits; but "though hand join in hand, the wicked shall not go unpunished" (Pr 11:21).

A young man in our Bible Institute in Chicago got on the streetcar, and before the conductor came around to take the fare, they reached the Institute, and he jumped off without paying his fare. In thinking over that act he said: "That was not just right. I had my ride, and I ought to pay the fare."

He remembered the face of the conductor, and he went to the car barns and paid him the five cents.

"Well," the conductor said, "you are a fool not to keep it."

"No," the young man said, "I am not. I got the ride, and I ought to have paid for it."

"But it was my business to collect it."

"No, it was my business to hand it to you."

The conductor said, "I think you must belong to that Bible Institute."

I have heard few things said of the Institute that pleased me so much as that one thing. Not long after that the conductor came to the Institute and asked the student to come to see him. A cottage meeting was started in his house; and not only himself but a number of others around there were converted as a result of that one act.

You can hardly take up a paper now without reading of some cashier of a bank who has become a defaulter, or of some large swindling operation that has ruined scores, or of some breach of trust, or fraudulent failure in business. These things are going on all over the land.

I would to God that we could have all gambling swept away. If Christian men take the right stand, they can check it and break it up in a great many places. It leads to stealing.

Where the Stream Starts

The stream generally starts at home and in the school. Parents are woefully lax in their condemnation and punishment of the sin of stealing. The child begins by taking sugar, it may be. The mother makes light of it at first, and the child's conscience is violated without any sense of wrong. By and by it is not an easy matter to check the habit, because it grows and multiplies with every new commission.

The value of the thing that is stolen has nothing to say to the guilt of the act. Two people were once arguing upon this point, and one said: "Well, you will not contend that a theft of a pin and of a dollar are the same to God?" "When you tell me the difference between the value of a pin and of a dollar to God," said the other, "I will answer your question."

The value or amount is not what is to be considered, but whether the act is right or wrong. Partial obedience is not enough: obedience must be entire.

The little indulgences, the small transgressions are what drive religion out of the soul. They lay the foundation for the grosser sins. If you give way to little temptations, you will not be able to resist when great temptations come to you.

GOD'S WEIGHTS

Extortioner, are you ready to step into the scales? What will you do with the condemnation of God— "Thou hast taken usury and increase, and thou hast greedily gained of thy neighbors by extortion, and hast forgotten me, saith the Lord God" (Eze 22: 12)?

Employer, are you guilty of sweating your employees? Have you defrauded the hireling of his wages? Have you paid starvation wages? "Thou shalt not oppress an hired servant that is poor and needy, whether he be of thy brethren, or of thy strangers that are in thy land within thy gates (Deu 24:14). What mean ye that ye beat my people to pieces, and grind the faces of the poor? saith the Lord God of hosts (Is 3:15). Behold, the hire of the laborers who have reaped down your fields, which is of you kept back by fraud, crieth: and the cries of them which have reaped are entered into the ears of the Lord of sabaoth" (Ja 5:4).

And you, *employee,* have you been honest with your employer? Have you robbed him of his due by wasting your time when he was not looking? If God should summon you into His presence now, what would you say?

Let the *merchant* step into the scales. See if you will prove light when weighed against the law of

God. Are you guilty of adulterating what you sell? Do you substitute inferior grades of goods? Are your advertisements deceptive? Are your cheap prices made possible by defrauding your customers either in quantity or in quality? Do you teach your clerks to put a French or an English tag on domestic manufactures, and then sell them as imported goods? Do you tell them to say that the goods are all wool when you know they are half cotton? Do you give short weight or measure? See what God says in His Word: "Shall I count them pure with the wicked balances, and with the bag of deceitful weights?" (Mic 6:11); "Thou shalt not have in thy bag divers weights, a great and a small: thou shalt not have in thy house divers measures, a great and a small. But thou shalt have a perfect and just weight, a perfect and just measure shalt thou have: that thy days may be lengthened in the land which the LORD thy God giveth thee" (Deu 25:13-16).

"Ye shall do no unrighteousness in judgment, in meteyard, in weight, or in measure. Just balances, just weights, a just ephah and a just hin, shall ye have" (Lev 19:35-36). Are you like those who said: "When will the new moon be gone, that we may sell corn? and the sabbath, that we may set forth wheat, making the ephah small, and the shekel great, and falsifying the balances by deceit? that we may buy the poor for silver, and the needy for a pair of shoes; yea, and sell the refuse of the wheat?" (Amos 8:5-6).

"Show me a people whose trade is dishonest," said Froude, "and I will show you a people whose religion is a sham." Unless your religion can keep you honest in your business, it isn't worth much; it isn't the right kind. God is a God of righteousness, and no true follower of His can swerve one inch to the right or left without disobeying Him.

STOLEN GOODS A BURDEN

I heard of a boy who stole a cannonball from a navy yard. He watched his opportunity, sneaked into the yard, and secured it. But when he had it, he hardly knew what to do with it. It was heavy, and too large to conceal in his pocket, so he had to put it under his hat. When he got home with it, he dared not show it to his parents, because it would have led at once to his detection. He said in after years it was the last thing he ever stole.

The story is told that one of Queen Victoria's diamonds valued at six-hundred thousand dollars was stolen from a jeweler's window, to whom it had been given to set. A few months afterward a miserable man died a miserable death in a poor lodging-house. In his pocket was found the diamond and a letter telling how he had not dared to sell it lest it lead to his discovery and imprisonment. It never brought him anything but anxiety and pain.

Everything you steal is a curse to you in that way. The sin overreaches itself. A man who takes money that does not belong to him never gets any lasting comfort. He has no real pleasure, for he has a guilty conscience. He cannot look an honest man in the face. He loses peace of mind here, and all hope of heaven hereafter. "As the partridge sitteth on eggs, and hatcheth them not; so he that getteth riches, and not by right, shall leave them in the midst of his days, and at his end shall be a fool" (Jer 17:11). "That no man go beyond and defraud his brother in any matter: because that the Lord is the avenger of all such" (1 Th 4:6).

I may be speaking to some clerk who perhaps took five cents today out of his employer's drawer to buy a cigar; perhaps he took ten cents to get a shave, and thinks he will put it back tomorrow—no one will ever know it. If you have taken a cent, you are a thief. Do you ever think how those little stealings may bring you to ruin? Let your employer find it out. If he doesn't take you into court, he will discharge you. Your hopes will be blasted, and it will be hard work to get up again. Whatever condition you are in, do not take a cent that does not belong to you. Rather than steal, go up to heaven in poverty—go up to heaven from the poorhouse. Be honest rather than go through the world in a gilded chariot of stolen riches.

RESTITUTION

If you have ever taken money dishonestly, you need not pray God to forgive you and fill you with the Holy Ghost until you make restitution. If you have not got the money now to pay back, will to do it, and God accepts the willing mind.

Many a man is kept in darkness and unrest because he fails to obey God on this point. If the plough has gone deep, if the repentance is true, it will bring forth fruit. What use is there in my coming to God until I am willing to make it good, like Zacchaeus, if I have done any man wrong or have taken anything from him falsely? "If the wicked restore the pledge, give again that he had robbed, walk in the statutes of life, without committing iniquity; he shall surely live, he shall not die. None of his sins that he hath committed shall be mentioned unto him" (Eze 33:15-16). Confession and restitution are the steps that lead up to forgiveness. Until you tread those steps, you may expect your conscience to be troubled, your sin to haunt you.

I was preaching in British Columbia some years ago, and a young man came to me and wanted to become a Christian. He had been smuggling opium into the States.

"Well, my friend," I said, "I don't think there is any chance for you to become a Christian until you make restitution." He said, "If I attempt to do that, I will fall into the clutches of the law, and I will go to the penitentiary." "Well," I replied, "you had better do that than go to the judgment-seat of God with that sin upon your soul, and have eternal punishment. The Lord will be very merciful if you set your face to do right."

He went away sorrowful, but came back the next day, and said: "I have a young wife and child, and all the furniture in my house I have bought with money I have got in this dishonest way. If I become a Christian, that furniture will have to go, and my wife will know it." "Better let your wife know it, and better let your home and furniture go." "Would you come up and see my wife?" he asked, "I don't know what she will say."

I went up to see her, and when I told her, the tears

trickled down her cheeks, and she said: "Mr. Moody, I will gladly give everything if my husband can become a true Christian."

She took out her pocketbook, and handed over her last penny. He had a piece of land in the United States, which he deeded over to the government. I do not know in all my backward track of any living man who has had a better testimony for Jesus Christ than that man. He had been dishonest, but when the truth came to him that he must make it right before God would help him, he made it right and then God used him wonderfully.

No amount of weeping over sin and saying that you feel sorry is going to help it unless you are willing to confess, and make restitution.

The Ninth Commandment

Thou shalt not bear false witness against thy neighbour.

Two out of the Ten Commandments deal with sins that find expression by the tongue—the third commandment, which forbids taking God's name in vain, and this ninth commandment, which forbids false witness against our neighbor. This twofold prohibition ought to impress us as a solemn warning, especially as we find that the pages of Scripture are full of condemnation of sins of the tongue. The Psalms, Proverbs, and the epistle of James deal largely with the subject.

Truth Necessary

Organized society of a degree higher than that of the herding of animals and flocking of birds depends so much upon the power of speech, that without it we may say society would be impossible. Language is an essential element in the social fabric. To fulfill its purpose it must be trustworthy. Words must command confidence. Anything which undermines the truth takes (as it were) the mortar out of the building, and if general, must mean ruin. Paul said, "Wherefore putting away lying, speak every man

99

truth with his neighbour: for we are members one
of another" (Eph 4:25). Note the reason given—
"we are members one of another." All community,
all union and fellowship would be shattered if a man
did not know whether to believe his neighbor or not.

The transgressions of this commandment are very
varied in form, and very frequent. Men and women
of all ages have to guard against them. They include
some of the most besetting sins. David said in his
haste, "All men are liars" (Ps 116:11). Someone
has remarked that if he had been living nowadays, he
might say it without haste and not be very far wide
of the truth.

PERJURY

The bearing of false witness is forbidden, but this
must not be limited merely to testimony given in the
law court or under oath. Isn't it a condemnation that
men have to be put under oath in order to make sure
of their speaking the truth? As a legal offense, perjury—the bearing of false witness when under
oath—is one of the most serious crimes that can be
committed. Nearly every civilized nation visits it
with heavy punishment. Unless promptly checked, it
would shake the very foundation of justice.

Lying—uttering or acting falsehood—and *slander*— the spreading of false reports tending to destroy the reputation of another—are two of the most
common violations of this commandment.

LYING

We have got nowadays so that we divide lies into
white lies and black lies, society lies, business lies,

etc. The Word of God knows no such letting-down of the standard. A lie is a lie, no matter what are the circumstances under which it is uttered, or by whom. I have heard that in Siam they sew up the mouth of a confirmed liar. I am afraid if that was the custom in America, a good many would suffer. Parents should begin with their children while they are young and teach them to be strictly truthful at all times. There is a proverb: "A lie has no legs." It requires other lies to support it. Tell one lie and you are forced to tell others to back it up.

SLANDER

You don't like to have anyone bear false witness against you, or help to ruin your character or reputation; then why should you do it to others? How public men are slandered in this country! None escape, whether good or bad. Judgment is passed upon them, their family, their character, by the press and by individuals who know little or nothing about them. If one-tenth that is said and written about our public men were true, half of them should be hung. Slander has been called "tongue murder." Slanderers are compared to flies that always settle on sores, but do not touch a man's good parts.

If the archangel Gabriel should come down to earth and mix in human affairs, I believe his character would be assailed inside of forty-eight hours. Slander called Christ a gluttonous man and a wine-bibber. He claimed to be the Truth, but instead of worshiping Him, men took Him and crucified Him.

When anyone spoke evil of another in the presence of Peter the Great, he used promptly to stop him, and say:

"Well, now, has he not got a bright side? Tell me what you know good of him. It is easy to splash mud, but I would rather help a man to keep his coat clean."

I need not stop to run through the whole catalog of sins that are related to these three. False rumor, exaggeration, misrepresentation, insinuation, gossip, equivocation, holding back of the truth when it is due and right to tell it, disparagement, perversion of meaning: these are common transgressions of this ninth commandment, differing in form and degree of guilt according to the motive or manner of their expression. They bear false witness against a man before the tribunal of public opinion—a court whose judgment none of us escapes. As so much of our life is passed in public view, any untruth that leads to a false judgment is a grievous wrong.

A TEST OF TRUE RELIGION

Government of the tongue is made the test of true religion by James. "If any man among you seem to be religious, and bridleth not his tongue, but deceiveth his own heart, this man's religion is vain" (Ja 1: 26). "For in many things we offend all. If any man offend not in word, the same is a perfect man, and be able also to bridle the whole body" (Ja 3:2). Just as a doctor looks at the tongue and can tell the condition of the bodily health, so a man's words are an index of what is within. Truth will spring from a good heart: falsehood and deceit from a corrupt heart. When Ananias kept back part of the price of the land, Peter asked him, "Why hath Satan filled thine heart to lie to the Holy Ghost" (Ac 5:3)? Satan is the father of lies and the promoter of lies.

FOR GOOD OR EVIL

The tongue can be an instrument of untold good or incalculable evil. Someone has said that a sharp tongue is the only edged tool that grows keener with constant use. "Thy tongue deviseth mischiefs; like a sharp razor, working deceitfully" (Ps 52:2); "They have sharpened their tongues like a serpent; adders' poion is under their lips" (Ps 140:3); "The mouth of a righteous man is a well of life: but violence covereth the mouth of the wicked" (Pr 10:11); "A wholesome tongue is a tree of life: but perverseness therein is a breach in the spirit" (Pr 15:4). Bishop Hall said that the tongues of busybodies are like the tails of Samson's foxes—they carry firebrands and are enough to set the whole field of the world in a flame.

"Behold, we put bits in the horses' mouths, that they may obey us; and we turn about their whole body. Behold also the ships, which though they be so great, and are driven of fierce winds, yet are they turned about with a very small helm, whithersoever the governor listeth. Even so the tongue is a little member, and boasteth great things. Behold, how great a matter a little fire kindleth! And the tongue is a fire, a world of iniquity: so is the tongue among our members, that it defileth the whole body, and setteth on fire the course of nature; and it is set on fire of hell.

"For every kind of beasts, and of birds, and of serpents, and of things in the sea, is tamed, and hath been tamed by mankind: but the tongue can no man tame; it is an unruly evil, full of deadly poison. Therewith bless we God, even the Father; and therewith curse we men, which are made after the similitude of God. Out of the same mouth proceedeth blessing and cursing. My brethren, these things ought not so to be. Doth a fountain send forth at the same place sweet water and bitter? Can the fig tree, my brethren, bear olive berries? either a vine, figs? so can no fountain both yield salt water and fresh. Who is a wise man and endued with knowledge among you? let him shew out of a good conversation his works with meekness of wisdom. But if ye have bitter envying and strife in your hearts, glory not, and lie not against the truth" (Ja 3:3-14).

Blighted hopes and blasted reputations are witness to its awful power. In many cases the tongue has murdered its victims. Can we not all recall cases where men and women have died under the wounds of calumny and misrepresentation? History is full of such cases.

WORDS NEVER CALLED BACK

The most dangerous thing about it is that a word once uttered can never be obliterated. Someone has said that lying is a worse crime than counterfeiting. There is some hope of following up bad coins until they are all recovered; but an evil word can never be overtaken. The mind of the hearer or reader has been poisoned, and human devices cannot reach in and cleanse it. Lies can never be called back.

A woman who was well known as a scandalmonger, went and confessed to the priest. He gave her a ripe thistle-top, and told her to go out and scatter the seeds one by one. She wondered at the penance, but obeyed; then she came and told the priest. He next told her to go and gather again the scattered seeds. Of course she saw that it was impossible. The priest used it as an object lesson to cure her of the sin of scandalous talk.

THE FATE OF THE LIAR AND SLANDERER

These sins are devilish, and the Bible is severe in its denunciations of them. It contains many solemn warnings. "Thou shalt destroy them that speak leasing: the LORD will abhor the bloody and deceitful man" (Ps 5:6); "The mouth of them that speak lies shall be stopped. Whoso privily slandereth his neighbour, him will I cut off" (Ps 101:5); "Lying lips are an abomination to the LORD: but they that deal truly are His delight" (Pr 12:22); "By thy words thou shalt be justified, and by thy words thou shalt be condemned" (Mt 12:37); "All liars, shall have their part in the lake which burneth with fire and brimstone: which is the second death" (Rev 21:8). "Whosoever loveth and maketh a lie" shall in no wise enter into the new Jerusalem (Rev 22:15).

HOW TO OVERCOME

"But, Mr. Moody," you say, "how can I check myself? How can I overcome the habit of lying and gossip?" A lady once said to me that she had got so into the habit of exaggerating, that her friends said they could never understand her.

The cure is simple, but not very pleasant. Treat it as a *sin*, and confess it to God and the man whom you have wronged. As soon as you catch yourself lying, go straight to the person and confess you have lied. Let your confession be as wide as your transgression. If you have slandered or lied about anyone in public, let your confession be public. Many a person says some mean, false thing about another in the presence of others, and then tries to patch it up by going to that person alone. That is not making restitution. I need not go to God with confession until I have made it right with that person, if it is in my power to do so; He will not hear me.

Hannah Moore's method was a sure cure for scandal. Whenever she was told anything derogatory of another, her invariable reply was: "Come, we will go ask if it be true."

The effect was sometimes ludicrously painful. The tale-bearer was taken aback, stammered out a qualification, or begged that no notice might be taken of the statement. But the good lady was inexorable. Off she took the scandalmonger to the scandalized to make inquiry and compare accounts.

It is not likely that anybody ventured a second time to repeat a gossipy story to Hannah Moore.

My friend, how is it? If God should weigh you against this commandment, would you be found wanting? "Thou shalt not bear false witness." Are you innocent or guilty?

The Tenth Commandment

Thou shalt not covet thy neighbour's house, thou shalt not covet thy neighbour's wife, nor his manservant, nor his maidservant, nor his ox, nor his ass, nor anything that is thy neighbour's.

IN THE TWELFTH CHAPTER of Luke, our Saviour lifted two danger signals. "Beware ye of the leaven of the Pharisees, which is hypocrisy" (v. 1), and "Take heed, and beware of covetousness" (v. 15).

The greatest dupe the devil has in the world is the hypocrite; but the next greatest is the covetous man, "for a man's life consisteth not in the abundance of the things which he possesseth" (Lk 12:15).

I believe this sin is much stronger now than ever before in the world's history. We are not in the habit of calling it a sin. In his first epistle to the Thessalonians Paul speaks of a "cloak of covetousness" (2:5). Covetous men use it as a cloak and call it prudence and foresight. Who ever heard it confessed as a sin? I have heard many confessions, in public and private, during the past forty years, but never have I heard a man confess that he was guilty of this sin. The Bible does not tell of one man who ever recovered from it, and in all my experience I do not recall many who have been able to shake it off after it had fastened on them. A covetous man or woman generally remains covetous to the very end.

We may say that covetous desire plunged the human race into sin. We can trace the river back from age to age until we get to its rise in Eden. When Eve saw that the forbidden fruit was good for food and that it was desirable to the eyes, she partook of it, and Adam with her. They were not satisfied with all that God had showered upon them, but coveted the wisdom of gods which Satan deceitfully told them might be obtained by eating the fruit. She saw, she desired, then she took! Three steps from innocence into sin.

A Searching Commandment

It would be absurd for such a law as this to be placed upon any human statute book. It could never be enforced. The officers of the law would be powerless to detect infractions. The outward conduct may be regulated, but the thoughts and intents of a man are beyond the reach of human law.

But God can see behind outward actions. He can read the thoughts of the heart. Our innermost life, invisible to mortal eye, is laid bare before Him. We cannot deceive Him by external conformity. He is able to detect the least transgression and shortcoming, so that no man can shirk detection. God cannot be imposed upon by the cleanness of the outside of the cup and the platter.

Surely we have here another proof that the Ten Commandments are not of human origin, but must be divine.

This commandment, then, did not, even on the

surface, confine itself to visible actions, as did the preceding commandments. Even before Christ came and showed their spiritual sweep, men had a commandment that went beneath public conduct and touched the very springs of action. It directly prohibited—not the wrong act, but the wicked desire that prompted the act. It forbade the evil thought, the unlawful wish. It sought to prevent—not only sin, but the desire to sin. In God's sight it is as wicked to set covetous eyes as it is to lay thieving hands upon anything that is not ours.

And why? Because if the evil desire can be controlled, there will be no outbreak in conduct. Desires have been called "actions in the egg." The desire in the heart is the first step in the series that ends in action. Kill the evil desire, and you successfully avoid the ill results that would follow upon its hatching and development. Prevention is better than cure.

We must not limit covetousness to the matter of money. The commandment is not thus limited; it reads, "Thou shalt not covet . . . anything." That word "anything" is what will condemn us. Though we do not join the race for wealth, have we not sometimes a hungry longing for our neighbor's goodly lands, fine houses, beautiful clothes, brilliant reputation, personal accomplishments, easy circumstances, comfortable surroundings? Have we not had the desire to increase our possessions or to change our lot in accordance with what we see in others? If so, we are guilty of having broken this law.

GOD'S THOUGHTS ABOUT COVETOUSNESS

Let us examine a few of the Bible passages that

bear down on this sin, and see what are God's thoughts about it.

"Know ye not that the unrighteous shall not inherit the kingdom of God? Be not deceived: neither fornicators, nor idolaters, nor adulterers, nor effeminate, nor abusers of themselves with mankind, nor thieves, *nor covetous,* nor drunkards, nor revilers, nor extortioners, shall inherit the kingdom of God" (1 Co 6:9-10, italics added).

Notice that the covetous are named between thieves and drunkards. We lock up thieves and have no mercy on them. We loathe drunkards and consider them great sinners against the law of God as well as the law of the land. Yet there is far more said in the Bible against covetousness than against either stealing or drunkenness.

Covetousness and stealing are almost like Siamese twins—they go together so often. In fact we might add lying, and make them triplets. The covetous person is a thief *in* the shell. The thief is a covetous person *out of* the shell. Let a covetous person see something that he desires very much; let an opportunity of taking it be offered; how very soon he will break through the shell and come out in his true character as a thief. The Greek word translated *covetousness* means "an inordinate desire of getting." When the Gauls tasted the sweet wines of Italy, they asked where they came from and never rested until they had overrun Italy.

"For this ye know, that no whoremonger, nor unclean person, nor covetous man, who is an idolater, hath any inheritance in the kingdom of Christ and of God" (Eph 5:5).

There we have the same truth repeated; but notice that covetousness is called idolatry. The covetous man worships mammon, not God.

"Moreover thou shalt provide out of all the people able men, such as fear God, men of truth, *hating covetousness;* and place such over them, to be rulers of thousands, and rulers of hundreds, rulers of fifties, and rulers of tens" (Ex 18:21, italics added).

Isn't it extraordinary that Jethro, the man of the desert, should have given this advice to Moses? How did he learn to beware of covetousness? We honor men today if they are wealthy and covetous. We elect them to office in church and state. We often say that they will make better treasurers just because we know them to be covetous. But in God's sight a covetous man is as vile and black as any thief or drunkard. David said: "The wicked boasteth of his heart's desire, and blesseth the covetous, whom the Lord abhorreth" (Ps 10:3). I am afraid that many who profess to have put away wickedness also speak well of the covetous.

A SORE EVIL

"He that loveth silver shall not be satisfied with silver; nor he that loveth abundance with increase: this is also vanity. When goods increase, they are increased that eat them: and what good is there to the owners thereof, saving the beholding of them with their eyes? The sleep of the labouring man is sweet, whether he eat little or much: but the abundance of the rich, will not suffer him to sleep. There is a sore evil which I have seen under the sun, namely, riches kept for the owners thereof to their hurt" (Ec 5:10-13).

Isn't that true? Is the covetous man ever satisfied with his possessions? Aren't they vanity? Does he have peace of mind? Don't selfish riches always bring hurt?

The folly of covetousness is well shown in the following extract : "If you should see a man that had a large pond of water, yet living in continual thirst, nor suffering himself to drink half a draught for fear of lessening his pond; if you should see him wasting his time and strength in fetching more water to his pond, always thirsty, yet always carrying a bucket of water in his hand, watching early and late to catch the drops of rain, gaping after every cloud, and running greedily into every mire and mud in hopes of water, and always studying how to make every ditch empty itself into the pond; if you should see him grow grey in these anxious labors, and at last end a thirsty life by falling into his own pond, would you not say that such a one was not only the author of his own disquiet, but was foolish enough to be reckoned among madmen? But foolish and absurd as this character is, it does not represent half the follies and absurd disquiets of the covetous man."

I have read of a millionaire in France who was a miser. In order to make sure of his wealth, he dug a cave in his wine cellar so large and deep that he could go down into it with a ladder. The entrance had a door with a spring lock. After a time, he was missing. Search was made, but they could find no trace of him. At last his house was sold, and the purchaser discovered this door in the cellar. He opened

it, went down, and found the miser lying dead on
the ground in the midst of his riches. The door must
have shut accidentally after him, and he perished
miserably.

A TEMPTATION AND A SNARE

"They that will be [that is, desire to be] rich fall
into temptation and a snare, and into many foolish
and hurtful lusts, which drown men in destruction
and perdition" (1 Ti 6:9).

The Bible speaks of the deceitfulness of two
things—"the deceitfulness of sin" and "the deceitfulness of riches." Riches are like a mirage in the desert which has all the appearance of satisfying and
lures the traveler on with the promise of water and
shade; but he only wastes his strength in the effort
to reach it. So riches never satisfy: the pursuit of
them always turns out a snare.

Lot coveted the rich plains of Sodom, and what
did he gain? After twenty years spent in that wicked
city, he had to escape for his life, leaving all his
wealth behind him.

What did the thirty pieces of silver do for Judas?
Weren't they a snare?

Think of Balaam. He is generally regarded as a
false prophet, but I do not find that any of his proph-
ecies that are recorded are not true; they have been
literally fulfilled. Up to a certain point his character
shone magnificently, but the devil finally overcame
him by the bait of covetousness. He stepped over a
heavenly crown for the riches and honors that Balak
promised him. He went to perdition backwards. His
face was set toward God, but he backed into hell.

He wanted to die the death of the righteous, but he did not live the life of the righteous. It is sad to see so many who know God miss everything for riches.

Then consider the case of Gehazi. There is another man who was drowned in destruction and perdition by covetousness. He got more out of Naaman than he asked for, but he also got Naaman's leprosy. Think how he forfeited the friendship of his master Elisha, the man of God! So today lifelong friends are separated by this accursed desire. Homes are broken up. Men are willing to sell out peace and happiness for the sake of a few dollars.

Didn't David fall into foolish and hurtful lusts? He saw Bathsheba, Uriah's wife, and she was "very beautiful to look upon," and David became a murderer and an adulterer. The guilty longing hurled him into the deepest pit of sin. He had to reap bitterly as he had sowed.

I heard of a wealthy German out West who owned a lumber mill. He was worth nearly two millions of dollars, but his covetousness was so great that he once worked as a common laborer carrying railroad ties all day. It was the cause of his death.

"And Achan answered Joshua, and said, Indeed I have sinned against the Lord God of Israel, and thus and thus have I done: When I saw among the spoils a goodly Babylonish garment, and two hundred shekels of silver, and a wedge of gold of fifty shekels weight, then *I coveted them,* and took them; and, behold, they are hid in the earth in the midst of my tent, and the silver under it" (Jos 7:20-21, italics added).

He saw—he coveted—he took—he hid! The

covetous eye was what led Achan up to the wicked deed that brought sorrow and defeat upon the camp of Israel.

We know the terrible punishment that was meted out to Achan. God seems to have set danger signals at the threshold of each new age. It is remarkable how soon the first outbreaks of covetousness occurred. Think of Eve in Eden, Achan just after Israel had entered the Promised Land, Ananias and Sapphira in the early Christian church.

A ROOT EXTRACTOR

"For the love of money is the root of all evil: which while some coveted after, they have erred from the faith, and pierced themselves through with many sorrows" (1 Ti 6:10).

The Revised Version translates it—"a root of all kinds of evil." This tenth commandment has therefore been aptly called a "root-extractor," because it would tear up and destroy this root. Deep down in our corrupt nature it has spread. No one but God can rid us of it.

Matthew tells us that the deceitfulness of riches chokes the Word of God. Like the Mississippi river, which chokes up its mouth by the amount of soil it carried down. Isn't that true of many businessmen today? They are so engrossed with their affairs that they have not time for religion. They lose sight of their soul and its eternal welfare in their desire to amass wealth. They do not even hesitate to sell their souls to the devil. How many a man says, "We must make money, and if God's law stands in the way, brush it aside."

The word "lucre" occurs five times in the New Testament, and each time it is called "filthy lucre."

"A root of all kinds of evil." Yes, because what will not men be guilty of when prompted by the desire to be rich? Greed for gold leads men to commit violence and murder, to cheat and deceive and steal. It turns the heart to stone, devoid of all natural affection, cruel, unkind. How many families are wrecked over the father's will! The scramble for a share of the wealth smashes them to pieces. Covetous of rank and position in society, parents barter sons and daughters in ungodly marriage. Bodily health is no consideration. The uncontrollable fever for gold makes men renounce all their settled prospects and undertake hazardous journeys—no peril can drive them back.

It destroys faith and spirituality, turning men's minds and hearts away from God. It disturbs the peace of the community by prompting to acts of wrong. Covetousness has more than once led nation to war against nation for the sake of gaining territory or other material resources. It is said that when the Spaniards came over to conquer Peru, they sent a message to the king, saying, "Give us gold, for we Spaniards have a disease that can only be cured by gold."

Dr. Boardman has shown how covetousness leads to the transgression of every one of the commandments, and I cannot do better than quote his words: "Coveting tempts us into the violation of the first commandment, worshiping mammon in addition to Jehovah. Coveting tempts us into a violation of the second commandment, or idolatry. The apostle Paul expressly identifies the covetous man with an idolater: 'Covetousness, which is idolatry.' Again: Coveting tempts us into violation of the third commandment, or sacrilegious falsehood: for instance, Gehazi, lying on the matter of his interview with Naaman the Syrian, and Ananias and Sapphira perjuring themselves in the matter of the communty of goods.

"Again: Coveting tempts us into the violation of the fourth commandment, or Sabbath-breaking. It is covetousness which encroaches on God's appointed day of sacred rest, tempting us to run trains for merely secular purposes, to vend tobacco and liquors, to hawk newspapers. Again: Coveting tempts us into the violation of the fifth commandment, or disrespect for authority; tempting the young man to deride his early parental counsels, the citizen to trample on civic enactments. Again: Covetousness tempts us into violation of the sixth commandment, or murder. Recall how Judas' love of money lured him into the betrayal of his divine Friend into the hand of His murderers, his lure being the paltry sum of, say, fifteen dollars.

"Again: Covetousness tempts us into the violation of the seventh commandment, or adultery. Observe how Scripture combines greed and lust. Again: Covetousness tempts us into the violation of the eighth commandment, or theft. Recall how it tempted Achan to steal a goodly Babylonish mantle, two hundred shekels of silver, and a wedge of gold of fifty shekels weight. Again: Covetousness tempts us into the violation of the ninth commandment, or bearing false witness against our neighbor. Recall how the covetousness of Ahab instigated his wife

Jezebel to employ sons of Belial to bear blasphemous
and fatal testimony against Naboth, saying, 'Thou
didst curse God and the king.' "

HOW TO OVERCOME

You ask me how you are to cast this unclean spirit
out of your heart? I think I can tell you.

In the first place, make up your mind that by the
grace of God you will overcome the spirit of selfishness. You must overcome it, or it will overcome you.
Paul said: "Mortify therefore your members which
are upon the earth; fornication, uncleanness, inordinate affection, evil concupiscence, and covetousness,
which is idolatry: for which things' sake the wrath of
God cometh on the children of disobedience" (Col
3:5-6).

I heard of a rich man who was asked to make a
contribution on behalf of some charitable object.
The text was quoted to him, "He that hath pity upon
the poor lendeth unto the LORD; and that which he
hath given will he pay him again" (Pr 19:17). He
said that the security might be good enough, but the
credit was too long. He was dead within two weeks.
The wrath of God rested upon him as he never expected.

If you find yourself getting very miserly, begin to
scatter, like a wealthy farmer in New York state I
heard of. He was a noted miser, but he was converted. Soon after, a poor man who had been burned
out and had no provisions, came to him for help. The
farmer thought he would be liberal and give the man
a ham from his smokehouse. On his way to get it,
the tempter whispered to him:

"Give him the smallest one you have."

He had a struggle whether he would give a large or a small ham, but finally he took down the largest he could find.

"You are a fool," the devil said.

"If you don't keep still," the farmer replied, "I will give him every ham I have in the smokehouse."

Mr. Durant told me he woke up one morning to find that he was a rich man, and he said that the greatest struggle of his life then took place as to whether he would let money be his master, or he be master of money; whether he would be its slave, or make it a slave to him. At last he got the victory, and that was how Wellesley College came to be built.

In the next place, cultivate the spirit of contentment. "Let your conversation be without covetousness; and be content with such things as ye have: for he hath said, I will never leave thee, nor forsake thee. So that we may boldly say, The Lord is my helper, and I will not fear what man shall do unto me" (Heb 13:5-6).

Contentment is the very opposite of covetousness, which is continually craving for something it does not possess. "Be content with such things as ye have" (Heb 13:5), not worrying about the future, because God has promised never to leave or forsake you. What does the child of God want more than this? I would rather have that promise than all the gold of the earth.

Would to God that we might be able to say with Paul, "I have coveted no man's silver, or gold, or apparel" (Ac 20:33). The Lord had made him partaker of His grace, and he was soon to be a partaker of His glory, and earthly things looked very small. "Godliness with contentment is great gain," he wrote to Timothy; "having food and raiment therewith let us be content" (1 Ti 6:6, 8). Observe that he puts godliness first. No worldly gain can satisfy the human heart. Roll the whole world in, and still there would be room.

May God tear the scales off our eyes if we are blinded by this sin. Oh, the folly of it, that we should set our heart's affections upon anything below! For we brought nothing into this world, and it is certain we can carry nothing out. "Be not thou afraid when one is made rich, when the glory of his house is increased; for when he dieth he shall carry nothing away: his glory shall not descend after him" (Ps 49:16-17).

The Handwriting Blotted Out

WE HAVE NOW CONSIDERED the Ten Commandments, and the question for each one of us is—are we keeping them? If God should weigh us by them, would we be found wanting or not wanting? Do we keep the law, the *whole* law? Are we obeying God with all our heart? Do we render Him a full and willing obedience?

ONE LAW, NOT TEN

These Ten Commandments are not ten different laws; they are one law. If I am being held up in the air by a chain with ten links and I break one of them, down I come, just as surely as if I break the whole ten. If I am forbidden to go out of an enclosure, it makes no difference at what point I break through the fence. "Whosoever shall keep the whole law, and yet offend in one point, he is guilty of all" (Ja 2:10). The golden chain of obedience is broken if one link is missing.

We sometimes hear people pray to be preserved from certain sins, as if they were in no danger of committing others. I firmly believe that if a man begins by willfully breaking one of these commandments it is much easier for him to break the others. I know of a gentleman who had a confidential clerk and insisted on his going down Sunday morning to work on his books. The young man had a good deal of principle, and at first refused; but he was anxious to keep in the good graces of his employer and finally yielded. He had not done that a great while before he speculated in stocks, and became a defaulter for one hundred and twenty thousand dollars. The employer had him arrested and put in the penitentiary for ten years, but I believe he was just as guilty in the sight of God as that young man, for he led him to take the first step on the downward road. You remember the story of a soldier who was smuggled into a fortress in a load of hay, and opened the gates to his comrades. Every sin we commit opens the door for other sins.

All Have Come Short

For fifteen hundred years man was under the law, and no one was equal to it. Christ came and showed that the commandments went beyond the mere letter; and can anyone since say that he has been able to keep them in his own strength? As the plummet is held up, we see how much we are out of the perpendicular. As we measure ourselves by that holy standard, we find how much we are lacking. As a child said, when reproved by her mother and told that she ought to do right: "How can I do right when there is no 'right' in me?" "All have sinned and come short of the glory of God" (Ro 3:23), "There is none righteous, no, not one" (Ro 3:10).

I do not say that all are equally guilty of gross violations of the commandments. It needs a certain amount of reckless courage openly to break a law, human or divine; but it is easy to *crack* them, as the child said. It has been remarked that the life of many professors of religion is full of fractures that result from little sins, little acts of temper and selfishness. It is possible to crack a costly vase so finely that it cannot be noticed by the observer; but let this be done again and again in different directions, and some day the vase will go to pieces at a touch. When we hear of someone who has had a lifelong reputation for good character and consistent living, suddenly falling into some shameful sin, we are shocked and puzzled. If we knew all, we would find that only the fall has been sudden, that he has been sliding toward it for years. Away back in his life we should find numerous *cracked* commandments. His exposure is only the falling of the vase to pieces.

FALSE WEIGHTS

Men have all sorts of weights that they think are going to satisfy, but they will find that they are altogether vanity, and lighter than vanity.

The moral man is as guilty as the rest. His morality cannot save him. "Except ye repent, ye shall all likewise perish" (Lk 13:3, 5). "Except ye be converted, and become as little children, ye shall not enter into the kingdom of heaven" (Mt 18:3). I have often heard good people say that our meetings were doing good, they were reaching the drunkards, and gamblers, and harlots; but they never realized that they needed the grace of God for themselves.

Nicodemus was probably one of the most moral men of his day. He was a teacher of the law. Yet Christ said to him: "Except a man be born again, he cannot see the kingdom of God." It is much easier to reach thieves and drunkards and vagabonds than self-righteous Pharisees. You do not have to preach to those men for weeks and months to convince them that they are sinners. When a man learns that he has need of God and that he is a sinner, it is very easy to reach him. But the self-righteous Pharisee needs salvation as much as any drunkard that walks the streets.

I read of a minister traveling in the South who obtained permission to preach in the local jail. A son of his host went with him. On the way back the young man who was not a Christian, said to the minister:

"I hope some of the convicts were impressed. Such a sermon as that ought to do them good."

"Did it do you good?" the minister asked.

"Oh, you were preaching to the convicts!" the young man answered.

The minister shook his head, and said: "I preached Christ, and you need Him as much as they."

If you do not repent of your sins and ask Him for mercy, there is no hope for you. Let me ask you to take this question home to yourself. If a summons should come at midnight for you to be "weighed in the balances," what would become of your soul?

Many are only making a profession. You belong to the church; but are you ready to be weighed— ready to step into the scales? A great many would be found like those five foolish virgins. When the hour came, they would be found with no oil in their lamps. If you have only an empty lamp, or are living on mere formalism, I beg of you to give it up. Give up that dead, cold, miserable lukewarmness. God will have none of it. Are you trusting to your good works? Do you think your Bible, your crucifix, your prayers, your church-going will help you?

Or do you set your hope upon your education, your wealth, your earthly distinctions? What will your university education amount to, and all your wealth and honors, if you go down through lust and passion and covetousness, and lose your soul at last? We are not redeemed with corruptible things as silver and gold but with the precious blood of Christ. If you have not Christ when God weighs you, "Tekel" will be your sentence.

Do not Despair

I can imagine that you are saying to yourself, "If we are to be judged by these laws, how are we going to be saved? Nearly every one of them has been broken by us—in spirit, if not in letter." I almost hear you say: "I wonder if Mr. Moody is ready to be weighed. Would he like to put those tests to himself?"

With all humility I reply that if God commanded me to step into the scales now, I am ready.

"What!" you say, "haven't you broken the law?"

Yes, I have. I was a sinner before God, the same as you; but forty years ago I pled guilty at His bar. I cried for mercy, and He forgave me. If I step into the scales, the Son of God has promised to be with me. I would not dare to step in without Him. If I did, how quickly the scales would fly up!

CHRIST IS ALL

Christ kept the law. If He had ever broken it, He would have to die for Himself; but because He was a Lamb without spot or blemish, His atoning death is efficacious for you and me. He had no sin of His own to atone for, and so God accepted His sacrifice. Christ is the end of the law for righteousness to everyone that believeth. We are righteous in God's sight, because the righteousness of God which is by faith in Jesus Christ is unto all and upon all them that believe.

If we had to live forever with our sins in the handwriting of God on the wall, it would be hell on earth. But thank God for the Gospel we preach! If we repent, our sins will all be blotted out. "You, being dead in your sins . . . hath he quickened together with him, having forgiven you all trespasses; blotting out the handwriting of ordinances that was against us, which was contrary to us, and took it out of the way, nailing it to his cross" (Col 2:13-14).

LOVE, THE FULFILLING OF THE LAW

If the love of God is shed abroad in your heart, you will be able to fulfill the law. Paul reduced the commandments to one: "Love is the fulfilling of the law" (Ro 13:10). Someone has written the following:

Love to God will admit no other God.
Love resents everything that debases its object
    by representing it by an image.
Love to God will never dishonor His name.
Love to God will reverence His day.
Love to parents makes one honor them.

Hate, not love, is a murderer.
Lust, not love, commits adultery.
Love will give, but never steal.
Love will not slander or lie.
Love's eye is not covetous.

ARE YOU READY?

It is the height of madness to turn away and run the risk of being called by God to judgment and have no hope in Christ. Now is the day and hour to accept salvation, and then He will be with you. Do you step aside and say: "I'm not ready yet. I want a little more time to prepare, to turn the matter over in my mind"? Well, you have time, but bear in mind it is only the present; you do not know that you will have tomorrow. Wasn't Belshazzar cut off suddenly? Would he have believed that that was going to be his last night, that he would never see the light of another sun? That banquet of sin didn't close as he expected. As long as you delay you are in danger. If you don't enter into the kingdom of heaven by God's way, you cannot enter at all. You must accept Christ as your Saviour, or you will never be fit to be weighed.

My friend, do you have Him? Will you remain as you are and be found wanting, or will you accept Christ and be ready for the summons? "This is the record, that God hath given to us eternal life, and this life is in His Son. He that hath the Son hath life: and he that hath not the Son of God hath not life" (1 Jn 5:11, 12).

May God open your heart to receive His Son now!